ITALIAN

**With menu decoder, survival
guide and two-way dictionary**

Thomas Cook
Publishing

www.thomascookpublishing.com

Introduction.......................5

Greetings...........................9

Eating out.........................13

Shopping..........................29

Getting around.................37

Accommodation................43

Survival guide................49

Emergencies....................59

Dictionary.......................63

Quick reference...............94

How to use this guide

The ten chapters in this guide are colour-coded to help you find what you're looking for. These colours are used on the tabs of the pages and in the contents on the previous page and above.

For quick reference, you'll find some basic expressions on the inside front cover and essential emergency phrases on the inside back cover. There is also a handy reference section for numbers, measurements and clothes sizes at the back of the guide.

Front cover photography © Bengt af Geijerstam / www.photolibrary.com
Cover design/artwork by Sharon Edwards
Photo credits: José A. Warletta (p9) and Ulrik De Wachter (p63)

Produced by The Content Works Ltd
www.thecontentworks.com
Design concept: Mike Wade
Layout: Tika Stefano
Text: Kathryn Tomasetti
Editing: Giovanna Dunmall & Amanda Castleman
Proofing: Wendy Janes
Project editor: Begoña Juarros
Management: Lisa Plumridge & Rik Mulder

Published by Thomas Cook Publishing
A division of Thomas Cook Tour Operations Limited
PO Box 227, Unit 18, Coningsby Road
Peterborough PE3 8SB, United Kingdom
Company Registration No 1450464 England
email: books@thomascook.com
www.thomascookpublishing.com
+44 (0)1733 416477

ISBN-13: 978-1-84157-673-2

First edition © 2007 Thomas Cook Publishing
Text © 2007 Thomas Cook Publishing

Project Editor: Kelly Pipes
Production/DTP: Steven Collins

Printed and bound in Italy by Printer Trento

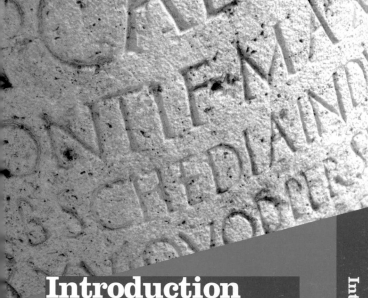

Introduction

Italian is a beautiful language, both melodic and expressive. It's fun and easy to get a grasp of common phrases and vocabulary, especially when you are surrounded by people willing to practice with you. Like any new skill, don't be afraid of making mistakes – Italians are a forgiving people, far happier to listen to a few stumbled words in Italian than a barrage of English. Once you get past the basics, you'll quickly realise that Italian is a joy to speak. Throw in a few gestures, and you may soon be mistaken for a local.

Introduction

Italian is a romance language, like French and Spanish, whose roots derive from ancient Latin. The Italian alphabet is made up of 21 letters – identical to the English alphabet, but without the letters j, k, w, x and y, which are only found in words borrowed from other languages.

Up until unification in 1861, Italy was made up of a number of city-states, each of which had its own language, or dialect. In order for different parts of the newly formed nation to communicate among themselves, an official language needed to be chosen. It was primarily due to the success of the **Divina Commedia** by Dante Alighieri, and **I Promessi Sposi** by Alessandro Manzoni, both written in Florentine, that this dialect from Tuscany was chosen as the official Italian language. However, it was only towards the middle of the 20th century, with mandatory schooling, that modern-day Italian actually became the most prolific language in Italy. Dialects are still spoken today (which is why you may have more difficulty understanding the locals in different areas), but, sadly, they are often considered 'crude', and are not taught to children. If this trend continues, many local dialects will be entirely lost.

Reading and writing Italian is relatively simple, once you master a few basic rules, as all words are spelled exactly as they are pronounced (unlike French, or even English).
- The letters c and g, when preceding the letters i and e, are pronounced 'ch' and 'j', respectively. When they precede

Is that a see-deh-car?
Don't be surprised to hear everyday English words included in Italian – unlike French, the Italian language is constantly adopting foreign words, like T-shirt, babysitter, computer, trendy and even sidecar!

any other letters, they are pronounced as 'k' and 'gh'.
- The letter g is not pronounced when placed before either an n or an l, and results instead in the sounds 'nya' and 'lya'.
- The letter z is generally pronounced as a 'ts' sound.
- The letter s is pronounced as in English if it's a double s, but generally as a 'z' sound when it occurs alone.
- H is the only letter in written Italian that does not have a sound of its own, but is used instead to change the pronunciation of other letters (like c and g, above), or is silently placed at the beginning of a word.

Sentences are generally ordered subject followed by verb, for example '**Io mangio una frittata**' (I eat an omelette). However, because verbs are conjugated according to the subject, the subject is often dropped. So it's entirely acceptable, and much more common, to say '**Mangio una frittata**', the conjugation of **mangiare**, to eat, denoting that it is the first person (me) doing the eating.

The easiest way to formulate questions is simply through inflecting your voice. Raising your tone at the end of a phrase transforms a statement into a question, with no need to rearrange words. For example, '**Mangio una frittata?**' – same word arrangement as above – means 'Should I eat an omelette?'.

To conjugate a regular verb, take the infinitive – the "to do" form listed in the dictionary – and lop off the last three letters:

parl-are   to speak

Then add the appropriate ending:

io parl-o	I speak
tu parl-i	you speak
lui/lei parl-a	he/she speaks
noi parl-iamo	we speak
voi parl-ate	you speak (plural)
loro parl-ano	they speak

By following the above guidelines, along with the essential phrases included in this book, you should be able to make yourself understood, and grasp most of what's going on around you. **Buon viaggio!**

Basic conversation

Hello	**Buongiorno/ Salve/Ciao**	*bwonjohrnoh/ sahlveh/chow*
Goodbye	**Arrivederci/ Ciao**	*ahreevehdehrchee/ chow*
Yes	**Sì**	*see*
No	**No**	*no*
Please	**Per favore**	*pehr fahvohreh*
Thank you	**Grazie**	*grahtsyeh*
You're welcome	**Prego**	*prehgoh*
Sorry	**Mi dispiace**	*mee deespyahche*
Excuse me (apology)	**Scusami**	*skoozahmee*
Excuse me (to get attention)	**Scusi**	*skoozee*
Excuse me (to get past)	**Scusi/Permesso**	*skoozee/ pehrmehsoh*
Do you speak English?	**Parla/Parli inglese?**	*parlah/parlee een-glehseh?*
I don't speak Italian	**Non parlo italiano**	*non parloh eetahlyahnoh*
I speak a little Italian	**Parlo un pò d'italiano**	*parloh oon poh de tahlyahnoh*
What?	**Cosa?**	*kohzah?*
I understand	**Capisco**	*kahpeeskoh*
I don't understand	**Non capisco**	*non kahpeeskoh*
Do you understand?	**Capisce/i?**	*kahpeesheh/ee?*
I don't know	**Non lo so**	*non loh soh*
I can't	**Non posso**	*non pohsoh*
Can you... please?	**Può/Puoi... per favore?**	*pwoh/pwoyee... pe fahvohreh?*
- speak more slowly	- **parlare più lentamente**	- *parlahreh pyoo lentahmehnteh*
- repeat that	- **ripeterlo**	- *reepehterloh*

Greetings

Other than the hugely touristy central areas of Florence, Venice and Rome, most Italians speak little English. However, if you manage to master a few of the basics, you'll receive far more compliments than you deserve! This is especially true if you are spending your holiday in one area, as Italians tend to take a neighbourhood approach to life. Try going to the same bar a couple of mornings in a row, and you can bet that by the third day, the **barista** will know your order, the locals will know where you are from, and you'll have more than a few opportunities to practise your Italian.

Meeting someone

Hello	**Buongiorno/ Salve**	*bwohnjohrnoh/salve*
Hi	**Ciao**	*chow*
Good morning	**Buongiorno**	*bwohnjohrnoh*
Good afternoon	**Buon pomeriggio**	*bwohn pomehreejyo*
Good evening	**Buona sera**	*bwohnah sehrah*
Sir/Mr	**Signore/Sig.**	*seenyohreh*
Madam/Mrs	**Signora/Sig.ra**	*seenyohrah*
Miss	**Signorina/Sig.na**	*seenyohreenah*
How are you?	**Come sta/stai?**	*komeh stah/sty?*
Fine, thank you	**Bene, grazie**	*behneh, gratsyeh*
And you?	**E lei/tu?**	*eh lay/too?*
Very well	**Molto bene**	*molto behneh*
Not very well	**Non tanto bene**	*non tahntoh behneh*

Cin-cin!

In the land of superstition, the practice of toasting comes laden with extra luck-promoting guidelines. Make sure to look directly into the eyes of the person with whom you are clinking glasses, and never ever clink across other people's arms!

Small talk

My name is...	**Mi chiamo...**	*mee kyahmoh...*
What's your name?	**Come si chiama?/**	*kohmeh see kyahma*
	Come ti chiami?	*/kohmeh tee kyahm*
I'm pleased to meet you	**Piacere**	*pyachehreh*

Where are you from?	**Da dove viene/vieni?**	da _dohveh_ _vyehneh/vyehnee?_
I am from Britain	**Vengo dalla Gran Bretagna**	_vengoh dallah gran brehtahnya_
Do you live here?	**Abita/abiti qui?**	_ahbeetah/ahbeetee kwee?_
This is a great...	**Questo è... fantastico/a**	_kwehstoh eh... fantahsteekoh/ah_
- country	**- un paese**	- _oon pahehzeh_
- city/town	**- una città**	- _oonah cheetah_
I am staying at...	**Sto all'...**	_stoh ahl..._
I'm just here for the day	**Sono qui solo per la giornata**	_sono kwee sohloh pehr la johrnahtah_
I'm in... for...	**Sono a... per...**	_sono ah... pehr..._
- a weekend	**- il fine settimana**	- _eel feeneh sehteemahnah_
- a week	**- una settimana**	- _oonah sehteemahnah_
How old are you?	**Quanti anni ha/ hai?**	_kwahnteeh ahnnee ah/ay?_
I'm... years old	**Ho... anni**	_oh... ahnnee_

Family

This is...	**Le/ti presento...**	_leh/tee prehzentoh..._
my husband	**- mio marito**	- _meeyoh mahreetoh_
my wife	**- mia moglie**	- _meeyah mohlyeh_
my partner	**- il mio compagno/ la mia compagna**	- _eel meeyoh kompahnyoh/lah meeyah kompahnyah_
my boyfriend/ girlfriend	**- il mio ragazzo/la mia ragazza**	- _eel meeyoh rahgahtsoh/lah meeyah rahgahtsah_
have...	**Ho...**	_oh..._
a son	**- un figlio**	- _oon feelyoh_
a daughter	**- una figlia**	- _oonah feelyah_
a grandson	**- un nipote**	- _oon neepohteh_
a granddaughter	**- una nipote**	- _oonah neepohteh_
Do you have...	**Ha/Hai...**	_ah/ay..._
children?	**- figli?**	- _feelyee_
grandchildren?	**- nipoti?**	- _neepohtee?_

11

I don´t have children	**Non ho figli**	*non oh feelyee*
Are you married?	**È/Sei sposato/a?**	*eh/say spozatoh/ah*
I´m...	**Sono...**	*sono...*
- single	**- celibe/nubile**	*- cheleebeh/noobeele*
- married	**- sposato/a**	*- spozatoh/ah*
- divorced	**- divorziato/a**	*- deevortsyatoh/ah*
- widowed	**- vedova/o**	*- vehdohvah/oh*

Saying goodbye

Goodbye	**Arrivederci**	*ahreevehderchee*
Good night	**Buona notte**	*bwohnah nohteh*
Sleep well	**Dorme/i bene**	*dohrmeh/eeh behneh*
See you later	**A più tardi**	*ah pyoo tahrdee*
Have a good trip	**Buon viaggio**	*bwohn vyahjyoh*
It was nice meeting you	**È stato un piacere conoscerla/ conoscerti**	*eh stahtoh oon pyachereh kohnosherla/ kohnoshertee*
Have fun	**Divertiti**	*deeverteetee*
Good luck	**In bocca al lupo**	*een bohkah ahl loop*
Keep in touch	**Teniamoci in contatto**	*tenyamohchee een kontahtoh*

Kiss me quick

In Italy, a quick kiss on each cheek is the standard greeting between family members, friends, acquaintances and sometimes even colleagues. Be prepared, as saying hello or goodbye to a large group can be quite a lengthy process!

Eating out

It seems like a stereotype, but nothing characterises the Italian culture better than food. And Italians love to swap recipes and discuss meals, as well as eat. The most common question Italians ask each other after travelling outside Italy is, "But how was the food?" As a result, mealtimes may very well be the most important hours of the day, and food preparation is taken extremely seriously. Stumble into almost any local **trattoria** and you are pretty much guaranteed an excellent meal. Try to hit the spots that are frequented by local families, a sure sign that the food will be traditional, rather than touristy.

Introduction

Unlike many other European countries, in Italy it is rare to find a restaurant that offers continuous service throughout the day – lunch and dinner hours are strictly adhered to. During the week, most restaurants serve a midday meal between 12.30pm and 3pm, and dinner from 8pm until 11pm or midnight. On the weekend these hours tend be slightly extended.

I'd like a...	**Vorrei un...**	*vohray oon...*
- table for two	**- tavolo per due persone**	*- tahvohloh pehr dooeh pehrsohne*
- sandwich	**- panino**	*- pahneenoh*
- coffee	**- caffè**	*- kahfeh*
- tea (with milk)	**- tè (con latte)**	*- teh (kon lahteh)*
Do you have a menu in English?	**Avete un menù in inglese?**	*ahvehteh oon mehno een eenglehseh?*
The bill, please	**Il conto, per favore**	*eel kontoh, pehr fahvohreh*

You may hear...

Fumatori o non-fumatori?	*foomahtohree oh non-foomahtohree?*	Smoking or non-smoking?
Che cosa prende/te?/ Avete scelto?	*keh kohsah prehndeh/teh?/ ahvehteh sheltoh?*	What are you going to have?

The cuisines of Italy

National specialities

Italian cuisine is fresh, tasty and most importantly, still based on seasonal produce. Make the most of year-round classics, like pasta or pizza, with seasonal touches, like wild asparagus in spring, chestnut and pumpkin in the autumn, or spiny artichokes during the chilly winter. The best dishes allow the pure flavours of every ingredient to shine through.

Signature dishes

(see the Menu decoder for more dishes)

Pasta	*pahstah*	Pasta
Pizza	*peetsah*	Pizza
Risotto	*reezohtoh*	Creamy rice dish
Polenta	*pohlehntah*	Cornmeal mush
Gelato	*jehlahtoh*	Ice-cream

Sicily

Sicily, the largest island in the Mediterranean, is said to be the birthplace of the goddess Venus. And who could fault her, with cuisine like this? While Sicily uses much of the same ingredient base as the rest of Italy, the results are uniquely different. Traces of former conquerors –Greek, Arab, Roman, Norman and Spanish – all shine through in the regional recipes.

Signature dishes
(see the Menu decoder for more dishes)

Caponata	*kahpohnahtah*	Eggplant appetiser
Arancini di riso	*ahrahncheenee dee reezoh*	Fried balls of rice, stuffed with meat and/or cheese
Pasta con le sarde	*pahstah kon leh sahrdeh*	Pasta with a sardine sauce
Pesce spada e calamari in teglia	*pehsheh spahdah eh kahlahmahree een tehlyah*	Swordfish and squid, cooked in wine with vegetables
Cannoli	*kahnohlee*	Crisp sweet biscuit tubes
Granita	*grahneetah*	Fruit-flavoured crushed ice

Course etiquette
You are not required to order every course – most people don't! However, do note that ordering two **primi** in a row, such as pasta followed by rice, is frowned upon.

Piedmont

Located in the northwest corner of Italy, Piedmont is famous for its musky ingredients and rich recipes. Mushrooms, pumpkin, salamis and even chocolates abound, as well as a huge variety of excellent wines, like Barolo and Barbaresco. The best time to visit is during October, when Alba hosts its world-famous yearly truffle festival.

Bagna cauda	_bah_nyah _kow_dah	Garlic and anchovy sauce
Fonduta	fohn_doo_tah	Melted fontina cheese
Fettuccine al tartufo	fehtoo_chee_neh ahl tahr_too_foh	Pasta with butter and truffles
Stracotto	strah_koh_toh	Slow-cooked beef and vegetables
Panna cotta	_pah_nah _koh_tah	Cooked cream with fruit coulis

Tuscany

Tuscany was home to Pellegrino Artusi, the author of **Kitchen Science and the Art of Eating Well**, published in 1891. This book is credited with creating modern Tuscan cuisine, as Artusi sifted through the rich and poor recipes of the region, and collected only the very best. The balance continues today, marrying simple ingredients with magnificent results!

No doggie bags
In Italy, the concept of doggie bags does not exist, and the only take-away food you can normally get from a restaurant is a pizza. Portions tend to be just the right size, making leftovers rare!

Signature dishes
(see the Menu decoder for more dishes)

Arrosto ubriaco all'acciuga	ah_rohs_toh oobree_ah_koh ahl-ah_choo_gah	Roasted veal with anchovies
Crostini	kroh_stee_nee	Toasted bread with toppings
Spaghetti aglio, olio e peperoncino	spah_geh_tee _ahl_yoh _ohl_yoh eh peh-pehrohn_chee_noh	Spaghetti with a garlic, olive oil and chilli pepper sauce
Scottiglia	skoh_tee_lyah	Rabbit, lamb and vegetables
Torta di riso	_tohr_tah dee _ree_zoh	Rice cake with candied fruits

Emilia-Romagna

Emilia-Romagna is known throughout Italy for its cuisine. Home to **parmiggiano reggiano** (Parmesan cheese), **prosciutto di parma** (Parma ham) – try it with melon slices or figs – and **aceto balsamico di Modena** (balsamic vinegar from Modena), the best homemade pasta also comes from this region. Allow plenty of time to eat, as meals are nothing if not lingering!

Signature dishes
(see the Menu decoder for more dishes)

Porcini in insalata	*pohrcheenee een eensahlahtah*	Salad of raw sliced **porcini** mushrooms
Piadine romagnole	*pyahdeeneh rohmahnyohleh*	Folded and grilled sandwiches
Tortelli di erbetta	*tohrtehlee dee ehrbehtah*	Pasta, stuffed with ricotta and Swiss chard
Anolini in brodo	*ahnohleenee een brohdoh*	Tiny meat-stuffed pasta served in a meat-based broth
Cotechino	*kohtehkeenoh*	Pork sausage served with lentils

Veneto

The Veneto cuisine is based primarily on local fish, many of which may seem unusual for British taste buds, such as eel or anchovies. Give them a try, and you'll probably be pleasantly surprised! Stop by the Rialto fish market in Venice to check out the ingredients first-hand – locals have been shopping for their fish on this same site for over 600 years.

Signature dishes
(see the Menu decoder for more dishes)

Risi e bisi	_reezee eh beezee_	Rice with bacon and peas
Alici al profumo di alloro	_ahleechee ahl prohfoomoh dee ahlohroh_	Anchovies cooked in lemon, garlic and bay leaves
Fegato alla veneziana	_fehgahtoh ahlah vehnehtsyahnah_	Liver cooked Venetian-style, with onions
Anguilla al forno	_ahngweelah ahl fohrnoh_	Oven-roasted eel
Crema fritta alla veneziana	_krehmah freetah ahlah vehnehtsyahneh_	Creamy, fried lemon and candied fruit

What is the coperto?

The **coperto** is a standard charge (usually a couple of euros) for all sit-down meals, which covers the cost of laundering the tablecloth and napkins, the bread, and sometimes a little taster.

Wine, beer & spirits

Italy is home to a massive range of excellent wines, and every region has a host of local specialities, all particular to the grapes, soil and weather conditions of the zone. But within the last ten years, Italians have also started to truly appreciate cocktail culture – don't miss the enormous happy hour spreads set out by trendy bars, particularly in Milan, where this new tradition started.

Prosecco	_Prohsehkoh_	fizzy white wine
Negroni	_Nehgrohnee_	Campari, gin and vermouth

Limoncello	*Leemohnchehloh*	*lemon liqueur (for after-dinner)*
Sambuca	*Sambookah*	*liquorice digestivo*
Grappa	*Grahpah*	*strong grape digestivo*

Could I have...?	**... per favore?**	*... pehr favohreh?*
- a beer	**- una birra**	*- oonah beerah*
- a glass/a bottle of white/red/ rosé wine	**- un bicchiere/ una bottiglia di vino bianco/ rosso/rosato**	*- oon beekyehreh/ oonah bohteelyah dee veenoh byankoh/ rohsoh/rohzahtoh*
- a glass/a bottle of champagne /prosecco	**- un bicchiere/ una bottiglia di champagne/ prosecco**	*- oon beekyehreh/ oonah bohteelyah dee shampahnyeh/ prohsehkoh*

You may hear...

Che cosa Le porto?	*keh kohsah leh pohrtoh?*	What can I get you?
Come lo vuole?	*kohmeh loh vwohleh?*	How would you like it?

Coffee culture

Ask for a coffee with your meal, and you might as well drape a foreign flag around your shoulders. Coffee is drunk only after a meal, for digestion, and then only an espresso!

Snacks & refreshments

Italians don't tend to be big snackers. An afternoon break may consist of a coffee, while children are indulged with sweet biscuits or a slice of foccaccia. Your best bet for a tasty snack on the go is to stop into a panetteria, or local bakery, where you'll find sweet and savoury treats specific to the area you are visiting.

Un caffè (macchiato)	*oon kahfeh (mahkyahtoh)*	An espresso (with a splash of milk)
Un cappuccino	*oon kahpoocheenoh*	Milky, foamy coffee
Un pezzo di foccaccia	*oon pehtsoh dee fohkahcha*	A salty, oily bread from Liguria

19

| Un panzerotto | *oon pahntsehrohtoh* | Bread with tomato and cheese |
| Le pizzette | *leh peetsehteh* | Miniature pizzas |

Vegetarians & special requirements

I'm vegetarian	**Sono vegetariano/a**	*sohnoh vehjehtaryah-noh/ah*
I don't eat...	**Non mangio...**	*non mahnjoh...*
- meat	**- carne**	*- kahrneh*
- fish	**- pesce**	*- pehsheh*
What's in this?	**Che cosa c'è dentro?**	*keh kohsah che dehntroh?*
I'm allergic...	**Sono allergico/a...**	*sohnoh ahlehrjeekoh/ah...*
- to nuts	**- ai noci**	*- ay nohchee*
- to wheat	**- al frumento**	*- ahl froomehntoh*
- to dairy	**- ai latticini**	*- ay lahteecheenee*

Digestion obsession

Italians are very concerned with proper digestion. An easy and acceptable way to explain eating preferences (for example, a vegetarian's choice not to eat meat) is to say you can't digest it!

Children

| Do you have a children's menu? | **Avete un menù bambini?** | *ahvehteh oon mehnoo bambeenee?* |
| What dishes are good for children? | **Quali sono i piatti adatti per bambini?** | *kwahlee sono ee pyahtee ahdahtee pehr bambeenee?* |

Menu decoder

Essentials

Breakfast	**La prima colazione**	*lah preemah kohlahtsyohneh*
Lunch	**Il pranzo**	*eel prahntsoh*
Dinner	**La cena**	*lah chenah*
Cover charge	**Il coperto**	*eel kohpehrtoh*
VAT inclusive	**IVA inclusa**	*eevah eenkloosah*
Service included	**Servizio incluso**	*sehrveetsyoh eenkloosoh*
Credit cards (not) accepted	**Le carte di credito (non) sono accettate**	*leh kahrteh dee krehdeetoh (non) sohnoh ahchetahteh*
First course	**Il primo**	*eel preemoh*
Second course	**Il secondo**	*eel sehkohndoh*
Dessert	**Il dolce**	*eel dohlche*
Dish of the day	**Il piatto del giorno**	*eel pyahtoh dehl johrnoh*
House specials	**Le specialità della casa**	*leh spechaleetah dehlah kahzah*
Set menu	**Il menù fisso**	*eel mehnoo feesoh*
A la carte menu	**Il menù à la carte**	*eel mehnoo ah lah kahrteh*
Tourist menu	**Il menù turistico**	*eel mehnoo tooreesteekoh*
Wine list	**La carta dei vini**	*lah kahrtah day veenee*
Drinks menu	**Il menù bevande**	*eel mehnoo behvahndeh*
Snack menu	**Il menù degli spuntini**	*eel mehnoo dehlyee spoonteenee*

Methods of preparation

Baked	**Al forno**	*ahl fohrnoh*
Boiled	**Lesso/bollito**	*lehsoh/bohleetoh*
Braised	**Brasato**	*brahzahtoh*
Breaded	**Impanato**	*eempahnahtoh*
Deep-fried	**Fritto in olio abbondante**	*freetoh een ohlyoh ahbondahnteh*
Fresh	**Fresco**	*frehskoh*
Fried	**Fritto**	*Freetoh*

21

Poisonous tomatoes?

Tomatoes, one of the staples of the Italian diet, were believed to be poisonous and grown purely as a decorative plant for hundreds of years. It was only during the 1800s that they became a popular addition to Italian cuisine.

Frozen	**Surgelato**	*soorjeh<u>lah</u>toh*
Grilled/broiled	**Grigliato**	*gree<u>lyah</u>toh*
Marinated	**Marinato**	*mahree<u>nah</u>toh*
Mashed	**Purè**	*poo<u>reh</u>*
Poached	**Bollito**	*boh<u>lee</u>toh*
Raw	**Crudo**	*<u>proo</u>doh*
Roasted	**Arrostito**	*ahroh<u>stee</u>toh*
Salty	**Salato**	*sah<u>lah</u>toh*
Sautéed	**Trifolati/in tegame**	*treefoh<u>lah</u>tee/een teh<u>gah</u>meh*
Smoked	**Affumicato**	*ahfoomee<u>kah</u>toh*
Spicy (flavour)	**Speziato**	*speh<u>tsyah</u>toh*
Spicy (hot)	**Piccante**	*pee<u>kahn</u>teh*
Steamed	**Al vapore**	*ahl vah<u>poh</u>reh*
Stewed	**Stufato**	*stoo<u>fah</u>toh*
Stuffed	**Ripieno**	*reep<u>yeh</u>noh*
Sweet	**Dolce**	*<u>dohl</u>che*
Rare	**Al sangue**	*ahl <u>sahng</u>weh*
Medium	**Medio cotto**	*<u>meh</u>dyoh <u>koh</u>toh*
Well done	**Ben cotto**	*behn <u>koh</u>toh*

Common food items

English	Italian	Pronunciation
Beef	Il manzo	*eel mahntsoh*
Chicken	Il pollo	*eel pohloh*
Turkey	Il tacchino	*eel tahkeenoh*
Lamb	L'agnello	*lahnyehloh*
Pork/roast pork	Carne di maiale/la porchetta	*karneh dee mahyahleh/lah pohrkehtah*
Seafood	I frutti di mare	*ee frootee dee mahreh*
Fish	Il pesce	*eel pehsheh*
Tuna	Il tonno	*eel tohnoh*
Beans	I fagioli	*ee fahjohlee*
Cheese	Il formaggio	*eel fohmahjoh*
Eggs	Le uova	*leh wohvah*
Lentils	Le lenticchie	*leh lehnteekyeh*
Pasta/noodles	La pasta	*lah pahstah*
Rice	Il riso	*eel reezoh*
Cabbage	La verza/il cavolo	*lah vehrtsah/eel kahvohloh*
Carrots	Le carote	*leh kahrohteh*
Cucumber	Il cetriolo	*eel chetreeohloh*
Garlic	L'aglio	*lahlyoh*
Mushrooms	I funghi	*ee foonghee*
Olives	Le olive	*leh ohleeveh*
Onion	La cipolla	*lah cheepohlah*
Potato	La patata	*lah pahtahtah*
Red/green pepper	Il peperone rosso/verde	*eel pehpehrohneh rohsoh/vehrdeh*
Tomato	Il pomodoro	*eel pohmohdohroh*
Vegetables	Le verdure	*leh vehrdooreh*
Bread	Il pane	*eel pahneh*
Oil	L'olio	*lohlyoh*
Pepper	Il pepe	*eel pehpeh*
Salt	Il sale	*eel sahleh*
Vinegar	L'aceto	*lahchehtoh*
Cake	La torta	*lah tohrtah*
Cereal	Il cereale	*eel cherehahleh*
Cream	La panna	*lah pahnah*
Fruit	La frutta	*lah frootah*
Ice-cream	Il gelato	*eel jehlahtoh*

Milk	Il latte	*eel lahteh*
Tart	La crostata	*lah krohstahtah*

Popular sauces

Amatriciana	*ahmahtreechahnah*	Tomato, bacon, chilli pepper and pecorino cheese
Carbonara	*kahrbohnahrah*	Bacon, egg and Parmesan cheese (no cream!)
Pesto	*pehstoh*	Basil, pine nuts, garlic and Parmesan cheese
Pomodoro	*pohmohdohroh*	Cooked tomatoes, with garlic and basil
Pomodoro fresco	*pohmohdohroh frehskoh*	Chopped raw tomatoes with garlic and basil
Ragù	*rahgoo*	Tomato and minced beef

Appetisers

Bruschetta	*brooskehtah*	Toasted bread topped with garlic, tomatoes and basil
Pinzimonio	*peentseemohnyoh*	Crudités served with a vinaigrette for dipping
Prosciutto e melone/fichi	*prohshootoh eh mehlohneh/ feechee*	Parma ham served with melon/fresh figs

Organic farms

Over a third of Italy's organic farms are located in Sicily. Until recent years, organic farming was partially subsidised by the state. These grants have now been reduced.

Eggs
Although eggs are rarely eaten at breakfast in Italy, they are prepared in a variety of ways at other mealtimes. **Uova in camicia** (poached), **frittate** (omelettes) and **uova sode** (boiled) are all favourites!

First course dishes

Anolini in brodo	*ahnohleenee een brohdoh*	Tiny, meat-stuffed pasta served in a meat-based broth
Burrida	*booreedah*	Traditional Sardinian fish stew
Fegato alla veneziana	*fehgahtoh ahlah vehnehtsyahnah*	Liver cooked Venetian-style, with onions
Fettuccine al tartufo	*fehtoocheeneh ahl tahrtoofoh*	Fettuccine pasta with butter and truffle shavings
Gnocchi alla romana	*nyohkee ahlah rohmahmah*	Large flat semolina dumplings, baked in the oven
Pasta al pesto, patate e fagiolini	*pahstah ahl pehstoh, pahtahteh eh fahjohleenee*	Pasta, potatoes and green beans, with a pesto sauce
Pasta con le sarde	*pahstah kon leh sahrdeh*	Pasta with a sardine sauce
Ribollita	*reebohleetah*	Tuscan white bean and bread stew
Risi e bisi	*reezee eh beezee*	Rice cooked with pancetta (similar to bacon) and peas
Risotto alla milanese	*reezohtoh ahlah meelahnehzeh*	A creamy saffron rice cooked in veal stock

25

Spaghetti aglio, olio e peperoncino	*spahgehtee ahlyoh ohlyoh eh peh-pehrohncheenoh*	Spaghetti with a garlic, olive oil and chilli pepper sauce
Tortelli di erbetta	*tohrtehlee dee ehrbehtah*	Squares of pasta stuffed with ricotta and Swiss chard

Second course dishes

Anguilla al forno	*ahngweelah ahl fohrnoh*	Oven-roasted eel
Bistecca alla Florentina	*beestehkah ahlah flohrehnteenah*	Grilled Chianina steak, cut at least two inches thick
Cotechino	*cohtehkeenoh*	A large pork sausage, often served with lentils
Fritto misto	*freetoh meestoh*	A big batch of mixed fried fish
Pesce spada e calamari in teglia	*pehsheh spahdah eh kahlahmahree een tehlyah*	Pan-cooked swordfish and squid
Scottiglia	*skohteelyah*	A main course of rabbit, lamb and braised vegetables
Stracotto	*strahkohtoh*	A slow-cooked beef and vegetable dish

Side dishes

Carciofi ripieni	*kahrchohfee reepyehnee*	Stuffed artichokes
Fiori di zucca fritti e mozzarella fritta	*fyohree dee zookah freetee eh moht-sahrehlah freetah*	Courgette flowers and mozzarella balls, breaded and deep fried
Fonduta	*fohndootah*	A creamy dish of melted fontina cheese
Insalata di puntarelle	*eensahlahtah dee poontahrehleh*	Raw chicory, anchovy and garlic salad
Insalata mista	*eensahlahtah meeztah*	Mixed green salad with grated carrots and tomatoes

Peperonata	*pehpehroh<u>nah</u>tah*	Peppers stewed in a tomato sauce

Desserts

Cannoli	*kah<u>noh</u>lee*	Sicilian deep-fried biscuit tubes, filled with ricotta
Cassata	*kah<u>sah</u>tah*	Sicilian cake made with ricotta and candied fruit
Crema fritta alla veneziana	*<u>kreh</u>mah <u>free</u>tah ahlah vehneh<u>tsyah</u>neh*	A creamy fried lemon and candied fruit dessert
Granita	*grah<u>nee</u>tah*	Fruit-flavoured crushed ice drink
Panna cotta	*<u>pah</u>nah <u>koh</u>tah*	Literally, cooked cream, served with a fruit coulis
Tiramisù	*teerahmee<u>soo</u>*	Coffee and liqueur-soaked biscuits with mascarpone
Torta di riso	*<u>tohr</u>tah dee <u>ree</u>zoh*	Rice cake with candied fruits

Grapple a Grappa

Distilled from wine-making leftovers – grape skins, stems and seeds – **Grappa** is sipped as an after-dinner digestive or added to an espresso for a **caffè corretto**.

Drinks

Birra	*<u>bee</u>rah*	Beer
Caffè (macchiato)	*kah<u>feh</u> (mah<u>kyah</u>toh)*	An espresso (with a splash of milk)
Cappuccino	*kahpoo<u>chee</u>noh*	A foamy milk coffee
Grappa	*<u>grah</u>pah*	A strong, clear digestivo made from grapes

Limoncello	*leemohn<u>cheh</u>loh*	A lemon liqueur for after dinner
Negroni	*neh<u>groh</u>nee*	An aperitivo made with Campari, gin and Vermouth
Prosecco	*proh<u>seh</u>koh*	Fizzy white wine, traditionally from the Veneto region
Sambuca	*sahm<u>boo</u>kah*	Aniseed-flavoured digestivo
Vino (rosso/ bianco/rosato)	*<u>vee</u>noh (<u>roh</u>soh/ <u>byahn</u>koh/roh<u>zah</u>toh)*	Wine (red/white/ rosé)

Snacks

Arancini di riso	*ahrahn<u>chee</u>nee dee <u>ree</u>zoh*	Fried balls of rice, stuffed with meat and/or cheese
Foccaccia	*foh<u>kah</u>cha*	A salty, oily bread from Liguria
Panzerotto	*pahntseh<u>roh</u>toh*	A doughy bread, filled with tomato and cheese
Piadine romagnole	*pyah<u>dee</u>neh rohmah<u>nyoh</u>leh*	Flat bread sandwiches, folded and grilled
Pizzette	*peet<u>seh</u>teh*	Miniature pizzas with pastry bases

Tiramisù!

The literal translation of **tiramisu** is "pick me up". Originating in Treviso (in the Veneto region), the dessert was said to be a favourite (and fortifying!) snack shared between lovers.

Shopping

Italy is truly a shopper's paradise. With designer clothes, luxurious linens, cutting-edge furniture and a wealth of antiques, you will find something that takes your fancy, and probably on numerous occasions throughout your trip. Bargaining is generally acceptable, especially at markets and for second-hand goods, but bear in mind that there is etiquette to be followed. Like a dance, don't force your way – smile, compliment, sigh, walk away. Play your cards right and you'll be strolling off with the object of your heart's desire, at much less than you thought you would be paying for it.

Essentials

Where can I buy...?	**Dove posso comprare...?**	*dohveh pohssoh komprahreh...?*
I'd like to buy...	**Vorrei comprare...**	*vohray komprahreh...*
Do you have...?	**Avete...?**	*ahvehteh...?*
Do you sell...?	**Vendete...?**	*vendehteh...?*
I'd like this	**Vorrei questo/a**	*vohray kwestoh/ah*
I'd prefer...	**Preferisco...**	*prehfehreeskoh...*
Could you show me...?	**Può farmi vedere...?**	*pwoh fahrmee vehdehreh...?*
I'm just looking, thanks	**Sto solo guardando, grazie**	*stoh sohloh gwardandoh, gratsyeh*
How much is it?	**Quanto costa questo?**	*kwahntoh kostah kwehstoh?*
Could you write down the price?	**Può scrivere il prezzo?**	*pwoh skreevehreh eel prehtsoh?*
Do you have any items on sale?	**Avete qualcosa in saldo?**	*ahvehteh kwahlkohzah een sahldoh?*
Could I have a discount?	**Può farmi lo sconto?**	*pwoh fahrmee loh skohntoh?*
Nothing else, thanks	**Basta così, grazie**	*bahstah kohzee, gratsyeh*

Opening hours

Most Italian shops are open Mon-Sat, from 10am-7.30pm, with a lunchtime break between 1pm and 3.30-4pm. Clothing and other stores in central and touristy areas do not close for lunch and supermarkets are open from 8.30am to 8 or 9pm (though most are closed on Sunday).

Do you accept credit cards?	**Accettate le carte di credito?**	*ahchetahteh leh kahrteh dee krehdeetoh?*
Could you post it to...?	**Può spedirlo a...?**	*pwoh spehdeerloh ah...?*
Can I exchange it?	**Posso scambiarlo?**	*pohssoh skambyahrloh?*
I'd like to return this	**Vorrei restituire questo/a**	*vohray restee-tooeereh kwestoh/ah*
I'd like a refund	**Vorrei un rimborso**	*vohray oon reemborsoh*

Exchange or refund?

Most stores will exchange your purchase within a certain time period (with receipt), but the possibility of a cash refund is truly one in a million. Ask before you buy!

Local specialities

Every corner of Italy has a local speciality, so be sure to leave plenty of room in your suitcase. Florence, Milan and Rome have the best designer shopping, and Naples, Sicily and Emilia-Romagna corner the food market with **pizza**, seafood and **parmigiano**, respectively. Make sure to ask for local recommendations wherever you are staying.

Can you recommend a shop selling local specialities?	**Può consigliarmi un negozio che vende delle specialità regionali?**	*pwoh konseelyahrmee oon nehgohtsyo keh vendeh dehleh spe-shahleetah rehjohnahlee?*
What should I buy from here?	**Che cosa dovrei comprare da qui?**	*keh kohzah dohvray komprahreh dah kwee?*

Is... (leather) good quality?	**(La pelle)... è di buona qualità?**	*(lah pehleh)... eh dee bwohnah kwahleetah*
Is it hand made?	**È stato fatto a mano?**	*eh stahtoh fahtoh a mahnoh?*
Can I order one?	**Posso ordinarne uno?**	*pohssoh ordeenahrne oonoh?*

Popular things to buy

Aceto balsamico	*ahchehtoh bahlsahmeekoh*	Balsamic vinegar from Modena
Carta Fiorentina	*kartah fyorenteenah*	Marbled paper products and stationery from Florence
Ceramiche artigianali	*cherahmeekeh ahrteejahnahlee*	Hand-made ceramics from Siena, Faenza and Deruta
Abbigliamento firmato	*ahbeelyahmentoh firmahtoh*	Designer clothes
Limoncello	*leemohnchehloh*	Lemon liqueur
Maschere di cartapesta	*mahskehreh dee kartahpehstah*	Traditional carnival masks from Venice
Olio d'oliva	*ohlyoh dohleevah*	Olive oil
Parmigiano reggiano	*pahrmeejahnoh rehjahnoh*	Parmesan cheese, from Emilia-Romagna
Pelletteria	*pehlehtehreeyah*	Leather goods
Pesto	*pehztoh*	Basil sauce from Liguria
Prosciutto di Parma	*prohshootoh dee pahrmah*	Parma ham
Vetro di Murano	*vehtroh dee moorahnoh*	Glass homeware/ jewellery made in Murano
Vino	*veenoh*	Wine

Clothes & shoes

Both clothing and shoes tend to be cheaper and more stylish than those found in the UK – although bear in mind that designer prices are expensive wherever you travel. Hit the area around **Via Montenapoleone** in central Milan for the best of the flagship stores, but save your cash for the sumptuous designer outlets dotted around Milan, Turin and Florence.

| Where is the... department? | **Dov'è? il reparto...** | *dohveh eel rehparto* |

- clothes	**- abbigliamento?**	- ahbeelyah<u>men</u>toh?
- shoe	**- scarpe?**	- <u>skar</u>peh?
- women's	**- donne?**	- <u>doh</u>neh?
- men's	**- uomo?**	- <u>woh</u>meeneeh?
- children's	**- bambini?**	- bam<u>bee</u>nee?
Which floor is the...?	**Su quale piano c'è il/la...?**	soo <u>kwah</u>leh pyah-noh che eel/lah...?

I'm looking for...	**Sto cercando...**	stoh cher<u>kan</u>doh...
- a skirt	**- una gonna**	- <u>oo</u>nah <u>goh</u>nah
- trousers	**- dei pantaloni**	- day pantah<u>loh</u>nee
- a top (jumper, blouse/shirt)	**- un pullover, una camicia**	- oon poo<u>loh</u>ver, <u>oo</u>nah kamee<u>tsch</u>ah
- a jacket	**- una giacca**	- <u>oo</u>nah <u>jah</u>kah
- a T-shirt	**- una maglietta**	- <u>oo</u>nah mah<u>lyeh</u>tah
- jeans	**- dei jeans**	- day jeans
- shoes	**- delle scarpe**	- <u>deh</u>leh <u>skar</u>peh
- underwear	**- della biancheria intima**	- <u>deh</u>lah byahnkeh<u>ree</u>-yah <u>een</u>teemah

Can I try it on?	**Posso provarlo/la?**	<u>poh</u>ssoh proh<u>var</u>loh/lah?
What size is it?	**Che taglia è?**	keh <u>tah</u>lyah eh?
My size is...	**Sono una taglia...**	<u>so</u>no <u>oo</u>nah <u>tah</u>lyah...
- small	**- piccola**	- <u>pee</u>kohlah
- medium	**- media**	- <u>meh</u>dyah
- large	**- grande**	- <u>gran</u>deh

(see clothes size conversion table on p.96 for full range of sizes)

Designer outlets
Stop by most major bookstores to pick up a copy of Theodora Van Meurs's **Lo Scoprioccasioni** (in English and Italian). This little guide lists all the major designer outlets in Italy – essential reading for the true fashionista.

33

Do you have this in my size?	**Ce l'avete nella mia taglia?**	che lahvehteh nehla meeyah tahlyah?
Where is the changing room?	**dove sono i camerini?**	_dohveh sono eeh kamereenee?_
It doesn't fit	**Non mi sta bene**	_non mee stah behneh_
It doesn't suit me	**Non è il mio stile**	_non eh eel meeyoh steeleh_
Do you have a... size?	**Ce l'avete in una taglia...**	che lahvehteh een oonah tahlyah...
- bigger	**- più grande?**	- pyoo grandeh?
- smaller	**- più piccola?**	- pyoo peekohlah?
Do you have it/them in...	**Ce l'avete/Ce li avete in...**	che lahvehteh/che lee ahvehteh een...
- black?	**- nero?**	- nehroh?
- white?	**- bianco?**	- byankoh?
- blue?	**- blue?**	- bloo?
- green?	**- verde?**	- vehrdeh?
- red?	**- rosso?**	- rohsoh?
Are they made of leather?	**Sono fatti/e di pelle?**	sono fahtee/eh dee pehleh?
I'm going to leave it/them	**Lo/li lascio**	loh/lee lahsho
I'll take it/them	**Lo/li prendo**	loh/lee prehndoh

Small change – an obsession

Cashiers will always ask if you have anything smaller than the denomination with which you are trying to pay. Don't be afraid of standing your ground, or you'll end up with only large notes,

You may hear...

Le posso aiutare?	leh pohsso hay-ootahreh?	Can I help you?
È già stato/a servito/a?	eh jah stahtoh/ah serveetoh/ah?	Have you been served?

Saldi

Standard sales periods, set by the Chamber of Commerce throughout all of Italy, are January 10 (or so) until mid-February and mid-July to mid-August – if you are bargain hunting, plan your trip accordingly!

Che taglia?	*keh tahlyah?*	What size?
Non ne abbiamo	*non neh ahbyahmoh*	We don't have any
Quacos'altro?	*kwahlkohzahltroh?*	Anything else?
Faccio un paccho regalo?	*facho oon pahkoh rehgahloh?*	Shall I wrap it for you?
Costa...	*kostah...*	It's...
(cinquanta) euro	*(cheenkwantah) ehuhro*	(50) euros
È scontato	*eh skontahtoh*	It's reduced

Where to shop

Where can I find...	**Dove posso trovare...**	*dohveh pohssoh trovahreh...*
- a bookshop?	**- una libreria?**	*- oonah leebrehreeyah?*
- a clothes shop?	**- un negozio di abigliamento?**	*- oon nehgohtsyo dee ahbeelyahmehntoh?*
- a department store?	**- un grande magazzino?**	*- oon grandeh mahgahtseenoh?*
- a gift shop?	**- un negozio di regali?**	*- oon nehgohtsyoh dee rehgahlee?*
- a market?	**- un mercato?**	*- oon mehrkahtoh?*
- a newsagent?	**- un'edicola?**	*- oon ehdeekohlah?*
- a shoe shop?	**- un negozio di scarpe?**	*- oon nehgohtsyoh dee skarpeh?*
- a tobacconist?	**- un tabacchaio?**	*- oon tahbahkayoh?*
- a souvenir shop	**- un negozio di souvenir?**	*- oon nehgohtsyoh dee souvenir?*

What's the best place to buy...?	**Dov'è il posto migliore per comprare...?**	dohveh eel pohstoh meelyohreh pehr komprahreh...?
I'd like to buy...	**Vorrei comprare...**	vohray komprahreh...
- a film	**- un film**	- oon feelm
- an English newspaper	**- un giornale inglese**	- oon johrnahleh eenglehseh
- a map	**- una pianta/ cartina**	- oonah pyantah/ karteenah
- postcards	**- dele cartoline**	- dehleh kartohleeneh
- stamps	**- dei francobolli**	- day frahnkohbohlee
- sun cream	**- della crema solare**	- dehlah krehmah sohlahreh

Food & markets

Is there a supermarket/ market nearby?	**C'è un supermercato/me rcato qui vicino?**	che oon soopehrmehrkah- toh/mehrkahtoh kwee veecheenoh?
Can I have...	**Posso avere...**	pohssoh ahvehreh...
- some bread?	**- del pane?**	- del pahneh?
- some fruit?	**- della frutta?**	- dehlah frootah?
- some cheese?	**- del formaggio?**	- del formahjoh?
- a bottle of water?	**- una bottiglia d'acqua?**	- oonah bohteelyah dahkwah?
I'd like... of that	**Vorrei... di quello**	vohray... dee kwehloh
- half a kilo	**- mezzo chilo**	- mehtsoh keeloh
- a small/big piece	**- un pezzo piccolo/grande**	- oon pehtsoh peekohloh/grandeh

Buongiorno!
It's common practice to greet staff in small stores by shouting out **buongiorno!** upon your entry – likewise, everyone will stop what they are doing and greet you in the same way!

Getting around

Times have changed since arrival in
Italy was equated with lost baggage,
crowds of impossibly enormous
shouting families, and thick clouds of
blue cigarette smoke. Smoking in
airports is now banned and baggage
normally arrives at the same time you
do, though demonstrative welcomes
remain a staple. Savour it – from the
clapping of airplane passengers upon
landing, to the gesticulating porters
and chatty taxi drivers, Italians are a
friendly, rambunctious, emotive people.
Throw yourself in and you'll be
embraced like a long lost relation.

Arrival

Being a peninsula, Italy's ports of entry are both numerous and varied. Hop on the high-speed train from Paris to Turin, cruise into Bari from Athens on the overnight ferry, or fly to virtually any city on a low-cost airline. If possible, try to plan where and how you'll be travelling onwards – the most convenient and cheapest travel options are not necessarily obvious upon arrival.

Where is/are...	**Dov'è/dove sono...**	*dohveh/dohveh sono...*
- the luggage from flight...?	**- i bagagli del volo...?**	*- ee bagalyee dehl vohloh?*
- the luggage trolleys?	**- i carrelli portabagagli?**	*- ee karelee portabagalyee?*
- the lost luggage office?	**- l'ufficio bagagli smarriti?**	*- loofeecho bagalyee zmareetee?*

Where is/are...	**Dov'è/dove sono...**	*dohveh/dohveh sono..*
- the buses?	**- gli autobus?**	*- lyee owtohboos?*
- the trains?	**- i treni?**	*- ee trehnee?*
- the taxis?	**- i taxi?**	*- ee tahxee?*
- the car rental?	**- l'autonoleggio?**	*- lowtonolehjoh?*
- the exit?	**- l'uscita?**	*- loosheetah?*
How do I get to hotel...?	**Come faccio ad arrivare all'albergo...?**	*kohmeh fachoh ad ahreevareh al albergo...?*

My baggage has been...	**Il mio bagaglio è stato...**	*il meeyoh bagalyoh eh stahtoh...*
- lost	**- perso**	*- perso*
- damaged	**- danneggiato**	*- dahnehjahtoh*
- stolen	**- rubato**	*- roobahtoh*

Customs

Customs officials in Italy fall into both extreme ends of the spectrum – either totally blasé, or meticulously thorough. Whatever the case, do your best to roll with the situation by following the locals. Be assertive if you feel you are being inappropriately questioned, but remain sweet and patient at all times.

The children are on this passport	**I bambini sono iscritti su questo passaporto**	*ee bambeenee sono eeskreetee soo kwehstoh pahsahpohrtoh*

We're here on holiday	**Siamo qui in vacanza**	_syamoh kwee een vahkantsah_
I'm going to...	**Vado a...**	_vado ah..._
I have nothing to declare	**Non ho niente da dichiarare**	_non oh nyenteh dah deekyararareh_
Do I have to declare this?	**Devo dichiarare questo?**	_dehvo deekyararareh kwehstoh?_

Tabacchi

Your local **tabacchaio** is the place to purchase stamps (**i francobolli**), bus tickets (**i biglietti per l'autobus**), pre-paid cards for parking (**le schede pre-pagate per parcheggiare**) and often a cup of coffee! Look out for shops with a large "T" above the door.

Car hire

Reservation desks for car hire are normally located just outside of the baggage claim in airports, or dotted around the area immediately surrounding train stations. You'll find internationally recognised brands such as Hertz and Avis, as well as a smattering of local agents (that may well be cheaper, especially if you haggle). If a car is essential transport for your trip, do your best to book before you arrive.

I'd like to hire a...	**Vorrei noleggiare una...**	_vohray nohlejahreh oonah..._
car	**- macchina**	_- mahkeenah_
people carrier	**- monovolume**	_- monovoloomeh_
with...	**con...**	_kon..._
air-conditioning	**- aria condizionata**	_- ahryah konditsyonahtah_
automatic transmission	**- cambio automatico**	_- kambyoh owtohmateeko_

How much is that for...	Quanto costa...	kwahntoh kostah...
- a day?	- al giorno?	- al johrnoh?
- a week?	- alla settimana?	- alla sehteemahnah?
Does that include mileage?	I chilometri sono compresi?	ee keelomehtree sono komprehzee?
Does that include insurance?	È compresa l'assicurazione?	eh komprehza lah-seekoorahtsyohneh?

On the road

Italians are excellent albeit extremely assertive drivers, but you can easily blend in if you obey a few basic rules. The left lane is for passing only. Pass quickly, and keep your indicator on to show you are passing. Don't be intimidated by drivers who drive too close. Most importantly, brush up on your speed-reading, as Italian road signs tend be posted in long lists!

What is the maximum speed?	Qual'è il limite di velocità?	kwaleh eel leemeeter dee vehlocheetah?
Can I park here?	Posso parcheggiare qui?	pohssoh parkehjahre kwee?
Where is the nearest petrol station?	Dov'è il distributore di benzina più vicino?	doveh eel deestree-bootoreh dee ben-zeenah pyoo veecheenoh?
Please fill up the tank with...	Per favore, riempia il serbatoio con...	pehr favohreh, reeempyah eel serba toyoh kon...
- unleaded	- benzina senza piombo	- benzeenah sentsah pyohmboh
- diesel	- gasolio/diesel	- gazohlyoh/deezehl
- leaded	- benzina con piombo	- benzeenah kon pyohmboh
- LPG	- GPL/gasauto	- geepee-el/gazowto

Directions

Is this the road to...?	Sono sulla strada giusta per...?	sono soohlah strah-dah joostah pehr...
How do I get to...?	Come faccio ad arrivare a...?	komeh facho ad ahreevareh ah...?
How far is it to...?	Quant'è distante...?	kwahnteh deestanteh.
How long will it take to get to...?	Quanto tempo ci vuole per arrivare a...?	kwahntoh tempoh chee vwaleh pehr areevareh ah...?

Could you point it out on the map?	**Me lo può indicare sulla piantina?**	*meh lo pwoh eendeekareh soola pyanteenah?*
I've lost my way	**Mi sono perso**	*mee sono pehrsoh*
On the right/left	**A destra/sinistra**	*ah destra/seeneestra*
Turn right/left	**Giri a destra/ sinistra**	*geeree ah destra/seeneestrah*
Straight ahead	**Diritto**	*deereetoh*
Turn around	**Tornare in dietro**	*tornahreh een dyehtroh*

The Vespa
Created in Genoa in the late 1940s, the Vespa (meaning 'wasp') is one of the most famous icons of Italian design. Rent one for chic sightseeing and stylish transport during your stay.

Public transport

Public transportation in Italy is exceptional in terms of accessibility and price, but sometimes frustrating in terms of frequency and punctuality (especially if you are off the highly popular or touristy main routes). Patience is a virtue, and nothing will teach you this lesson better than using the local system of trains, trams and buses. Stop by the tourist office for free maps, schedules, and general advice on getting around.

Bus	**Autobus**	*owtohboos*
Bus station	**Stazione autolinee**	*stahtsyohneh owtohlinyeh*
Train	**Treno**	*trehnoh*
Train station	**Stazione ferroviaria**	*stahtsyohneh fero- hvyareeah*

41

I would like to go to...	Vorrei andare a...	vohray andareh ah...
I would like a... ticket	Vorrei un biglietto di...	vohray oon beelyehtoh dee...
- single	- sola andata	- sola andata
- return	- andata e ritorno	- andata eh reetorno
- first class	- prima classe	- preema klahseh
- smoking/non-smoking	- fumatori/non-fumatori	- foomatohree/non-foomatohree

Taxis

I'd like a taxi to...	Vorrei un taxi per...	vohray oon tahxee pehr...
How much is it to...	Quant'è per andare...	kwahnteh pehr andareh...
- the airport?	- all'aeroporto?	- alaehrohpohrtoh?
- the town centre?	- in centro?	- een chentro?
- the hotel?	- all'albergo?	- alalbergo?

Tours

True stories about foreign couples settling in Italy, in combination with the allure the country has always had, means that almost any tour you can dream up probably exists. Wine-tasting in Tuscany, fresco-hunting in Umbria, cliff-climbing in Liguria – check what's available before you visit, as many of the more unusual tours may be difficult to find once you've arrived

Are there any organised tours of the town/region?	Ci sono delle gite organizzate della città/zona?	chee sono dehleh jeeteh organeetsahteh della cheetah/dzonah?
Where do they leave from?	Da dove partono?	da doveh partono?
What time does it start?	A che ora comincia?	ah keh orah komeencha?
Do you have English-speaking guides?	Avete delle guide che parlono inglese?	ahvehteh dehlch gweedeh keh parlono eenglehseh?
Is lunch/a snack included?	È incluso il pranzo/la merenda?	eh eenkloozo eel prahntsoh/lah merenda?
Do we get any free time?	Avremmo del tempo libero?	ahvrehmo dehl tehmpoh leebehro?

Accommodation

Accommodation varies immensely in Italy, but luckily the majority of places still have a family feel, whether it's a boutique hotel or a tiny **pensione**. The owner's granddaughter may direct you to her favourite beach, or the best **trattoria** will be (enthusiastically) pointed out to you, and more than likely it will be owned by someone's cousin/brother-in-law/oldest friend. Ask for tips – in general, Italians love to share their local expertise!

Wherever you choose to stay, don't forget to bring your passport. Show up without it and you'll probably be asked to head to the nearest **questura** (police station) for an official letter allowing you to book accommodation for the night – an exercise in bureaucracy you would not wish on your worst enemy!

Types of accommodation

Italian accommodation generally falls into four categories – hotels (**alberghi**), guesthouses (**pensioni**), Bed & Breakfasts, (with an emphasis on the bed, as Italian breakfasts tend to consist of a simple **brioche** or **cornetto** – a sweet croissant – and **cappuccino**), and country apartments/villas (**agriturismi**), often with working farms. If you are travelling off-season, make use of the town's tourist office, where you will be directed to unique places to stay, often only publicised locally.

I'd like to stay in...	**Vorrei stare in...**	*voray stareh een...*
- an apartment	- **un appartamento**	- *oon ahpartahmehnt*
- a campsite	- **un campeggio**	- *oon kampehjoh*
- a hotel	- **un albergo**	- *oon albergoh*
- a youth hostel	- **un ostello della gioventù**	- *oon ohstelloh dehla johventoo*
- a guest house	- **una pensione**	- *oonah penzyoneh*
- a country apartment/villa	- **un agriturismo**	- *oon agreetooreezm*
Is it...	**È...**	*eh...*
- full board?	- **pensione completa?**	- *penzyoneh komplehtah?*
- half board?	- **mezza pensione?**	- *mehtsa penzyoneh?*
- self-catering?	- **con cucina?**	- *kon koocheenah?*

Reservations

Do you have any rooms available?	**Avete delle camere libere?**	*ahvehteh dehleh kamehreh leebehreh?*
Can you recommend anywhere else?	**Mi può consigliare un'altro posto?**	*mee pwoh konsil-yareh oonaltro poc toh?*
I'd like to make a reservation for...	**Vorrei fare una prenotazione per...**	*voray fahreh oonah prehnotatsyoneh pehr...*
- tonight	- **questa notte**	- *kwestah nohteh*
- one night	- **una notte**	- *oonah nohteh*
- two nights	- **due notti**	- *dooeh nohtee*
- a week	- **una settimana**	- *oonah seteemahna*
From... (May 1st) to... (May 8th)	**Dal...(primo maggio) al/l'... (otto maggio)**	*dahl... (preemo mahjoh) ahl... (ohtoh mahjoh)*

Why are hotel keys so huge in Italy? It's standard practice to leave your room key at reception, and hotel owners often attach a huge brass keychain to the key to ensure that you do so. Err on the side of caution, and make sure all valuables are safely stowed or taken with you.

Room types

The definition of a standard room in Italy varies according to where exactly it is located (city, countryside, seaside), as well as how many stars the hotel has been assigned (between one, basic, and five, luxury). In lower-end accommodation and some of the most basic **pensioni,** don't count on a mini-bar, hairdryer or air-conditioning. Make sure to check in advance.

Do you have... room?	**Avete una camera...**	*ahvehteh oonah kamerah...*
- a single	**- singola?**	*- seengohlah?*
- a double	**- doppia?**	*- dohpyah?*
- with twin beds with...	**- a due letti con...**	*- ah dooeh lehtee? kon...*
- a cot?	**- una culla?**	*- oonah coolah?*
- a double bed?	**- un letto matrimoniale?**	*- oon lehtoh mahtreemonyaleh?*
- a bath/shower?	**- la vasca da bagno/ la doccia?**	*- lah vaska dah bahnyoh/lah docha?*
- air-conditioning?	**- l'aria condizionata?**	*- lahreea konditsyonahtah?*
- Internet access?	**- accesso internet?**	*- ahcheso eentehrnet?*
Can I see the room?	**Posso vedere la camera?**	*pohssoh vehdehreh lah kamehrah?*

Prices

Accommodation rates are usually very straightforward, and there are rarely hidden charges or additional taxes. Do beware of extremely expensive extras, like telephone fees or pay-per-view films. In swankier accommodation, you will be expected to tip the porter a few euros, and slipping a bill or two to the concierge can work miracles!

How much is...	**Quant'è...**	*kwahnteh...*
- a double room?	**- una camera doppia?**	*- oonah kamehrah dohpyah?*
- per night?	**- per notte?**	*- per nohteh?*
- per week?	**- per settimana?**	*- per sehteemahnah*
Is breakfast included?	**La prima colazione è inclusa?**	*lah preemah kolatsyoneh eh eenklooza?*
Do you have a reduction for children?	**Avete qualche sconto per i bambini?**	*ahvehteh kwalkeh skohntoh per ee bambeenee?*
Do you have a single room supplement?	**C'è un supplemento per la camera singola?**	*che oon sooplehmen toh per lah kamehra seengolah?*
I'll take it	**La prendo**	*lah prendoh*
Can I pay by...	**Posso pagare con...**	*pohssoh pahgahreh kon...*
- credit card?	**- la carta di credito?**	*- lah kartah dee kre deetoh?*
- traveller's cheque?	**- un assegno di viaggio/traveller's cheque?**	*- oon ahsehnyo dee vyajoh/travellers tscheck?*

Special requests

Could you...	**Può...**	*pwoh...*
- put this in the hotel safe?	**- mettere questo nella cassaforte dell'albergo?**	*- mehtehreh kwesto nehlah kasahforte dellalbergo?*
- order a taxi for me?	**- chiamarmi un taxi?**	*- kyamarmee oon tahxee?*
- wake me up at (7am)?	**- svegliarmi per le (sette)?**	*- svelyarmee per le (sehteh)?*

Can I have...	Posso avere...	_pohssoh ahvehreh..._
- a room with a sea view?	- una camera con vista sul mare?	- _oonah kamehrah kon veestah sool mahreh?_
- a bigger room?	- una camera più grande?	- _oonah kamehrah pyoo grandeh?_
- a quieter room?	- una camera più tranquilla?	- _oonah kamehrah pyoo trankweelah?_
Is there...	C'è...	_che..._
- a safe?	- una cassaforte?	- _oonah kasahforteh?_
- a babysitting service?	- il servizio baby-sitter?	- _eel serveetsyo babysitter?_
- a laundry service?	- il servizio lavanderia?	- _eel serveetsyo lah-vandehreeah?_
Is there wheelchair access?	È accessibile per le sedie a rotelle?	_eh ahchesseebeeleh pehr leh sehdyeh ah rohtelleh?_

Where's the iron?

Due to safety concerns, irons are generally not kept in hotel rooms in Italy. Ask to borrow one at reception - play your cards right and you may get your ironing done for you!

Checking in & out

have a reservation for tonight	Ho una prenotazione per questa notte	_oh oonah prehnotat-syoneh pehr kwest-ah nohteh_
n the name of...	A nome di...	_ah nohmeh dee..._
Here's my passport	Ecco il mio passaporto	_ehkoh eel meeyoh pahsahpohrtoh_

What time is check out?	**A che ora si deve lasciare libera la camera?**	*ah keh ohrah see dehveh lashareh leeberah lah kamehrah?*
Can I leave my bags here?	**Posso lasciare i miei bagagli qui?**	*pohssoh lashareh eeh myehee bahgahlyee kwee?*
I'd like to check out	**Vorrei fare il check-out**	*voray fahreh eel check-out*
Can I have the bill?	**Posso avere il conto?**	*pohssoh ahvehreh eel kontoh?*

Camping

Do you have...	**Avete...**	*ahvehteh...*
- a site available?	**- un sito libero?**	*- oon seetoh leebehroh?*
- electricity?	**- la corrente?**	*- lah korenteh?*
- hot showers?	**- delle doccie calde?**	*- dehleh doche kaldeh?*
- tents for hire?	**- delle tende da noleggiare?**	*- dehleh tendeh dah nolehjahreh?*
How much is it per...	**Quant'è per...**	*kwahnteh per...*
- tent	**- tenda?**	*- tendah?*
- caravan	**- roulotte?**	*- roolott?*
- person	**- persona?**	*- persohnah?*
- car	**- veicolo?**	*- veheekohloh?*

Agriturismi

While in Italy, don't miss the opportunity to stay at an **agriturismo** – working farms that produce robust wines, tangy olive oil and most of their own vegetables. The homemade treats make perfect gifts for friends and family back home!

Survival guide

Like in many Mediterranean countries, you don't want to dabble with bureaucracy in Italy. Be prepared for lines (or far more often, clumps), incomprehensible instructions and sometimes limited opening hours. Try to avoid banks, post offices and doctor's offices unless entirely necessary. Instead, try visiting the local pharmacy, as they often boast excellent and knowledgeable staff; use your debit card to withdraw cash from a **bancomat**; buy envelopes or make photocopies at a **cartoleria**. Frequent the many hole-in-the-wall shops in your neighbourhood – Italians are exceptional at small and personal service!

Money & banks

Where is the nearest...	Dov'è... più vicino/a?	dohveh... pyoo veecheenoh/ah?
- bank?	- la banca	- lah bahnkah
- ATM/bank machine?	- il bancomat	- eel bahnkohmat
- foreign exchange office?	- l'ufficio cambio	- loofeecho kahmby...
I'd like to...	Vorrei...	vohray...
- withdraw money	- prelevare dei soldi	- prehlehvahreh day soldee
- cash a traveller's cheque	- cambiare un assegno di viaggio/traveller's cheque	- kambyahreh oon ahsehnyoh dee vyajoh/travellers tscheck
- change money	- cambiare soldi	- kambyahreh soldee
- arrange a transfer	- fare un bonifico	- fahreh oon bohneefeekoh

Banks– are they ever open?

If you must visit an Italian bank, be sure to check its specific opening hours. Most banks are only open Mon-Fri, from approximately 8.30am-12.30pm, and for one hour and a half in the afternoon.

Could I have smaller notes, please?	Mi può dare banconote più piccole, per favore?	mee pwoh dahreh bahnkonohteh py... peekohleh, pehr fahvohreh?
What's the exchange rate?	Quant'è il tasso di cambio?	kwahnteh eel tahs... dee kambyoh?

What's the commission?	Quant'è la commissione?	kwahnteh lah komeesyoneh?
What's the charge for...	Quanto costa...	kwahntoh kostah...
- making a withdrawal?	- fare un prelievo?	- fahreh oon prehlyehvoh?
- exchanging money?	- cambiare soldi?	- kambyahreh soldee?
- cashing a cheque?	- cambiare un assegno?	- kambyahreh oon ahsehnyoh?
This is not right	Questo non è giusto	kwehstoh non eh joostoh
Is there a problem with my account?	C'è un problema con il mio conto?	che oon prohblehmah kon eel meeyoh kontoh?
The ATM/bank machine took my card	Il bancomat ha mangiato/trattenuto la mia carta	eel bahnkohmaht ah manjatoh/trahtehnootoh lah meeyah cartah
I've forgotten my PIN	Ho dimenticato il mio codice PIN	oh deementeekahtoh eel meeyoh kohdeeche peen

Post office

Where is the (main) post office?	Dov'è l'ufficio postale (centrale)?	dohveh loofeecho pohstahleh (chentrahleh)?
I'd like to send...	Vorrei spedire...	vohray spehdeereh...
- a letter	- una lettera	- oonah lehtehrah
- a postcard	- una cartolina	- oonah kartohleenah
- a parcel	- un pacchetto	- oon pahkehtoh
- a fax	- un fax	- oon fax
I'd like to send this...	Vorrei spedire questo...	vohray spehdeereh kwehstoh...
- to the United Kingdom	- in Gran Bretagna	- een gran bretahnyah
- by airmail	- via aerea	- veeyah ahehrehah
- by express mail	- con posta prioritaria	- kon pohstah preeohreetahryah
- by registered mail	- con posta raccomandata	- kon pohstah rahkohmahndahtah

51

I'd like...	**Vorrei...**	*vohray...*
- a stamp for this letter/postcard	**- un francobollo per questa lettera/cartolina**	*- oon frahnkohbohloh pehr kwehstah lehtehrah/kartohleenah*
- to buy envelopes	**- comprare delle buste**	*- komprahreh dehlleh boosteh*
- to make a photocopy	**- fare una fotocopia**	*- fahreh oonah fotohkohpyah*
It contains...	**Contiene...**	*kontyehneh...*
It's fragile	**È fragile**	*eh frahjeeleh*

Telecoms

| Where can I make an international phone call? | **Dove posso fare una telefonata internazionale?** | *dohveh pohssoh fahreh oonah tehlehfohnahtah eenternahtsyonahleh?* |
| Where can I buy a phone card? | **Dove posso comprare una scheda telefonica?** | *dohveh pohssoh komprahreh oonah skehdah tehlehfohneekah?* |

SIM cards vs schede telefoniche

You can buy a phone card (**una scheda telefonica**) from the local **tabacchaio**, but often it works out cheaper to buy a SIM card for your mobile phone, especially if you travel to Italy frequently.

| How do I call abroad? | **Come faccio a chiamare all'estero?** | *kohmeh facho ah kyahmahreh alestehroh?* |
| How much does it cost per minute? | **Quanto costa al minuto?** | *kwahntoh kostah a meenootoh?* |

The number is...	Il numero è...	*eel noomehroh eh...*
What's the area/country code for...?	Qual'è il prefisso per...?	*kwaleh eel pre-hfeesoh pehr...?*
The number is engaged	Il numero è occupato	*eel noomehroh eh ohkoopahtoh*
The connection is bad	La linea non è buona	*lah leenyah non eh bwohnah*
I've been cut off	La linea è caduta	*lah leenyah eh kah-dootah*
I'd like...	Vorrei...	*vohray...*
- a charger for my mobile phone	- un caricabatterie per il mio cellulare	*- oon kahreekah-bahtehreeyeh pehr eel meeyoh cheloolahreh*
- an adaptor plug	- un adattatore	*- oon ahdahtahtohreh*
- a pre-paid SIM card	- una carta SIM pre-pagata	*- oonah kartah seem prehpahgahtah*

Internet

Where's the nearest Internet café?	Dov'è l'internet caffè più vicino?	*dohvehleentehrnet kahfeh pyoo veecheenoh?*
Can I access the Internet here?	C'è modo di collegarmi a internet qui?	*che mohdoh dee kohlehgahrmee ah eentehrnet kwee?*
I'd like to...	Vorrei...	*vohray...*
use the Internet	- usare internet	*- oosahreh eentehrnet*
check my email	- controllare la mia email/posta elettronica	*- kontrohlahreh lah meeyah email/pohstah ehlehtrohneekah*
use a printer	- usare una stampante	*- oosahreh oonah stampahnteh*
How much is it...	Quanto costa...	*kwahntoh kostah...*
per minute?	- al minuto?	*- ahl meenootoh?*
per hour?	- all'ora?	*- ahlohrah?*
to buy a CD?	- comprare un CD?	*- komprahreh oon cheedee?*

How do I...	**Come faccio...**	_kohmeh facho..._
- log on?	**- a collegarmi?**	_- ah kohlehgahrmee_
- open a browser?	**- ad aprire il browser?**	_- ad ahpreereh eel browser?_
- print this?	**- a stampare questo?**	_- ah stampahreh kwehstoh?_
I need help with this computer	**Ho bisogno d'aiuto con questo computer**	_oh beezonyoh dah-yootoh kon kwehstoh kompyooter_
The computer has crashed	**Il computer si è bloccato**	_eel kompyooter see eh blohkahtoh_
I've finished	**Ho finito**	_oh feeneetoh_

Internet cafés

Recent regulations require you to present your passport or identity card in order to use the Internet at cafés or call centres. You may not be asked for it every time, but it's best to have it handy.

Chemist

Where's the nearest (all-night) pharmacy?	**Dov'è la farmacia (notturna) più vicina?**	_dohveh lah farmahcheeah (nohtoornah) pyoo veecheenah?_
What time does the pharmacy open/close?	**A che ora apre/chiude la farmacia?**	_ah keh ohrah ahpreh/kyoodeh lah farmahcheeah?_
I need something for...	**Ho bisogno di qualcosa per...**	_oh beezonyoh dee kwalkozah pehr..._
- diarrhoea	**- la diarrea**	_- lah deeahrehah_

- a cold	- il raffreddore	- eel rahfreh<u>doh</u>reh
- a cough	- la tosse	- lah <u>toh</u>seh
- sunburn	- la scottatura solare	- lah skota<u>too</u>rah soh<u>lah</u>reh
- motion sickness (car/sea)	- il mal di macchina/ mal di mare	- eel mahl dee <u>mah</u>keenah/<u>ma</u>reh
- hay fever	- il raffreddore da fieno	- eel rahfreh<u>doh</u>reh dah <u>fyeh</u>noh
- period pain	- i dolori menstruali	- ee doh<u>loh</u>ree mehnstroo<u>ah</u>lee
- abdominal pains	- i crampi addominali	- ee <u>kram</u>pee ahdohmee<u>nah</u>lee
- a urine infection	- un'infezione urinaria	- ooneenfeh<u>tsyo</u>neh ooree<u>nah</u>reeah
I'd like...	Vorrei...	voh<u>ray</u>...
- aspirin	- dell'aspirina	- dellaspee<u>ree</u>nah
- plasters	- dei cerotti	- day che<u>roh</u>tee
- condoms	- dei preservativi	- day prehzerva<u>tee</u>vee
- painkillers	- degli antidolorifici	- delyee ahntee-doh<u>loh</u><u>ree</u>feecheeh
How much should I take?	Quanto dovrei prendere?	<u>kwahn</u>toh doh<u>vray</u> <u>pren</u>dehreh?
Take...	Prendere...	<u>pren</u>dereh...
- a tablet	- una capsula	- <u>oo</u>nah kap<u>soo</u>lah
- a teaspoon	- un cucchiaino	- oon kookyah<u>ee</u>noh
- with water	- con acqua	- kon <u>ah</u>kwa
How often should I take this?	Quante volte al giorno lo/la devo prendere?	<u>kwahn</u>teh <u>vol</u>teh al <u>john</u>noh loh/lah <u>deh</u>voh <u>prehn</u>dehreh?
once/twice a day	- uno/due volte al giorno	- <u>oo</u>noh/<u>doo</u>eh <u>vol</u>teh al <u>john</u>noh
before/after meals	- primo/dopo i pasti	- <u>pree</u>moh/<u>doh</u>poh eeh <u>pah</u>stee
in the morning / evening	- la mattina/la sera	- lah mah<u>tee</u>nah/lah <u>seh</u>rah
Is it suitable for children?	È adatto per i bambini?	eh ah<u>dah</u>toh pehr ee bam<u>bee</u>nee?
Do I need a prescription?	Ho bisogno di una ricetta?	oh bee<u>zo</u>nyoh dee <u>oo</u>nah ree<u>che</u>tah?

| I have a prescription | **Ho una ricetta** | *oh oonah reechetah* |

Children

Where should I take the children?	**Dove dovrei portare i bambini?**	*dohveh dohvray pohrtahreh ee bambeenee?*
Where is the nearest...	**Dov'è... più vicino/a?**	*dohveh... pyoo veecheenoh/ah?*
- playground?	- **il campo giochi**	- *eel kampoh johkee*
- fairground?	- **il luna park**	- *eel loonah park*
- zoo?	- **lo zoo**	- *loh tsoh*
- swimming pool?	- **la piscina**	- *lah peesheenah*
- park?	- **il parco**	- *eel parkoh*
Is this suitable for children?	**Questo è adatto per i bambini?**	*kwehstoh eh ahdahtoh pehr ee bambeenee?*
Are children allowed?	**I bambini sono amessi?**	*ee bambeenee sono ahmehsee?*
Are there baby-changing facilities here?	**C'è una stanza per il cambio dei pannolini?**	*che oonah stahnsah pehr eel kambyoh day panohleenee?*
Do you have a...	**Avete un...**	*ahvehteh oon...*
- children's menu?	- **menù per i bambini?**	- *mehnoo pehr ee bambeenee?*
- high chair?	- **seggiolone?**	- *sehjohlohneh?*
Is there a...	**C'è un...**	*che oon...*
- child-minding service?	- **servizio di babysitter?**	- *sehrveetsyoh dee babyseetter?*
- nursery?	- **asilo nido?**	- *ahzeeloh needoh?*
Can you recommend a reliable babysitter?	**Può consigliarmi un babysitter affidabile?**	*pwoh konseelyarmi oon babyseetter ahfeedahbeeleh?*
He/she is... years old	**Ha... anni**	*ah... ahnee*
I'd like to buy...	**Vorrei comprare...**	*vohray komprahreh*
- nappies	- **i pannolini**	- *ee pahnohleenee*
- tissues	- **i fazzoletti**	- *ee fahtsolehtee*

Travellers with disabilities

I have a disability	Sono disabile	sono deezahbeeleh
I need assistance	Ho bisogno di assistenza	oh beezonyoh dee ahsistentsah
I am blind	Sono ciecho/cieca	sono chehkoh/kah
I am deaf	Sono sordo/a	sono sordoh/ah
I have a hearing aid	Ho un apparecchio acustico	oh oon ahpahrehkyoh ahkoosteekoh
I can't walk well	Non riesco a camminare bene	non reeyehskoh ah kahmeenahreh behneh
Is there a lift?	C'è un ascensore?	che oon ahshensohreh?
Is there wheelchair access?	C'è accesso per le sedie a rotelle?	che ahchehsoh pehr leh sehdyeh ah rohtehleh?
Can I bring my guide dog?	Posso portare il mio cane guida?	Pohsoh portahreh eel meeyoh kahneh gweedah?
Are there disabled toilets?	Ci sono i bagni per i disabili?	chee sono ee bahny-ee pehr ee deezahbeelee?
Do you offer disabled services?	Offrite servizi per i disabili?	ohfreeteh sehrveet-see pehr ee deezahbeelee?
Could you help me...	Può aiutarmi...	pwoh ahyootahrmee...
- cross the street?	- ad attraversare la strada?	- ad ahtrahvehrsahreh lah strahdah?
go up/down the stairs?	- a salire/scendere le scale?	- ah sahleereh/shendehreh leh skahleh?
Can I sit down somewhere?	C'è un posto dove posso sedermi?	che oon pohstoh dohveh pohsoh sehdehrme

Repairs & cleaning

This is broken	Questo/a è rotto/a	kwehstoh/ah eh rohtoh/ah
Can you fix it?	Me lo/a può aggiustare?	meh loh/ah pwoh ahjoostahreh?
Do you have...	Avete...	ahvehteh...
a battery?	- una batteria/pila?	- oonah bahtehree-ah/peelah?
spare parts?	- i pezzi di ricambio?	- ee pehtsee dee reekambyoh?

Can you... this?	Può... questo?	pwoh... kwehstoh?
- clean	- pulire	- pooleereh
- press	- stirare	- steerahreh
- dry-clean	- lavare a secco	- lahvahreh ah sehkoh
- patch	- ratmmendare	- rahmendahreh
When will it be ready?	Quando sarà pronto?	kwandoh sahrah prontoh?
This isn't mine	Questo/a non è mio/a	kwehstoh/ah non e meeyoh/ah

Tourist information

Where's the Tourist Information Office?	Dov'è l'Ufficio di Turismo?	dohveh loofeecho dee tooreesmoh?
Do you have a city/regional map?	Avete una pianta della città / regione?	ahvehteh oonah pyantah dehlah cheetah/rehjohne
What are the main places of interest?	Quali sono i luoghi principali da visitare?	kwahlee sono ee lwogee preencheepahlee dah veeseetahreh
Could you show me on the map?	Me lo può indicare sulla cartina?	meh loh pwoh een deekahreh soohla karteenah?
We'll be here for...	Saremo qui per...	syahmoh kwee pehr.
- half a day	- mezza giornata	- mehtsah johrnaht
- a day	- un giorno	- oon johrnoh
- a week	- una settimana	- oonah sehteemahn
Do you have a brochure in English?	Avete un depliant in inglese?	ahvehteh oon dehpleeant een eenglehseh?
We would like to go/do...	Vorremmo fare...	vohrehmoh fahreh.
- shopping	- shopping	- shopping
- hiking	- trekking	- trekking
- a scenic walk	- una passeggiata panoramica	- oonah pahsehjahtah pahnohrahmeeka
- a boat cruise	- una crociera	- oonah krohchehr
- a guided tour	- un tour guidato	- oon tour gweedaht
Are there any excursions?	Ci sono alcune escursioni?	chee sono alkoone ehzkoorzyohnee?

Emergencies

Pickpocketing is fairly common in larger Italian cities (particularly in Rome and Naples), and the preferred victims are tourists in highly crowded areas. Ensure that your valuables are safe at all times. This means never turning your back on your luggage or your purse, and keeping any handbags zipped up and locked firmly under your arm (some thieves may also try to snatch your bag off you as they ride past on their scooter). Make things easier for yourself by trying to look and behave as much like a local as possible. If you do have the misfortune to have your wallet stolen, block your credit cards immediately, and head to the nearest police station to make an official **denuncia**.

Medical

Where is the hospital?	**Dov'è l'ospedale?**	*dohveh lospehdahleh?*
I need...	**Ho bisogno di...**	*oh beezohnyoh dee...*
- a doctor	**- un medico**	*- oon mehdeekoh*
- a female doctor	**- una dottoressa**	*- oonah dohtohrehsa*
- an ambulance	**- un'ambulanza**	*- oonahmboolahntsah*
It's very urgent	**È molto urgente**	*eh mohltoh oorjehnte*
I'm injured	**Sono stato/a ferito/a**	*sono stahtoh/ah fehreetoh/ah*
Can I see the doctor?	**Posso vedere il medico?**	*pohssoh vehdehreh eel mehdeekoh?*
I don't feel well	**Non mi sento bene**	*non mee sentoh behneh*
I have...	**Ho...**	*oh...*
- a cold	**- un raffreddore**	*- oon rahfrehdohreh*
- diarrhoea	**- la diarrea**	*- lah deeahrayah*
- a temperature	**- la febbre**	*- lah fehbreh*
I have a lump here	**Ho un nodulo/ gonfiore qui**	*oh oon nohdooloh/ gonfyoreh kwee*
Can I have the morning-after pill?	**Posso avere la pillola del giorno dopo?**	*pohssoh ahvehreh lah peelohlah del johrnoh dohpoh?*
It hurts here	**Mi fa male qui**	*mee fah mahleh kwee*
It hurts a lot/a little	**Mi fa tanto male/ un po' male**	*mee fah tahntoh mahleh/oon poh mahleh*

Pain in the kidney?

In a country where health is often discussed ad nauseam, most Italians have an impressive knowledge of internal organs. Don't be surprised to hear the very common complaints of kidney pain or an aching liver!

| How much do I owe you? | **Quanto le devo?** | _kwahntoh leh dehvoh?_ |
| I have insurance | **Ho l'assicurazione** | _oh lahseekoorahtsy-ohneh_ |

Dentist

I need a dentist	**Ho bisogno di un dentista**	_oh beezohnyoh dee oon dehnteestah_
I have tooth ache	**Ho mal di denti**	_oh mahl dee dehntee_
This filling has fallen out	**Ho perso un'otturazione**	_oh pehrsoh oon-ohtoorahtsyohneh_
I have an abscess	**Ho un'ascesso**	_oh oonahshehssoh_
I've broken a tooth	**Ho un dente rotto**	_oh oon dehnteh rohtoh_
Are you going to take it out?	**Lo/la deve togliere?**	_loh/lah dehveh tolyehreh?_

Crime

I want to report a theft	**Voglio fare una denuncia di furto**	_volyoh fahreh oonah dehnooncha dee foortoh_
Someone has stolen my...	**Qualcuno ha rubato...**	_kwalkoonoh ah roobahtoh..._
bag	**- la mia borsa**	_- lah meeyah borsah_
car	**- la mia macchina**	_- lah meeyah mah-keenah_
credit cards	**- le mie carte di credito**	_- leh meeyeh karteh dee krehdeetoh_
money	**- i miei soldi**	_- ee myehee sohldee_
passport	**- il mio passaporto**	_- eel meeyoh pahsahpohrtoh_
I've been attacked	**Sono stato/a aggredito/a**	_sono stahtoh/ah ahgrehdeetoh/ah_

Lost property

I've lost my...	**Ho perso...**	_oh pehrsoh..._
car keys	**- le chiavi della macchina**	_- leh kyavee dehlah mahkeenah_
driving licence	**- la mia patente**	_- lah meeyah pahtenteh_
handbag	**- la mia borsa**	_- lah meeyah borsah_
flight tickets	**- i miei biglietti di aereo**	_- ee myehee beelye-htee dee ahehrehoh_

It happened... | È successo... | *eh soochehssoh...*
- this morning | - questa mattina | *- kwehstah mahteena*
- today | - oggi | *- ohjee*
- in the hotel | - nell'albergo | *- nehlalbergoh*
I left it in the taxi | L'ho lasciato nel taxi | *loh lahshatoh nel tahxee?*

Breakdowns

I've had... | Ho avuto... | *oh ahvootoh...*
- an accident | - un incidente | *- oon eencheedehnte*
- a breakdown | - un guasto | *- oon gwahstoh*
- a puncture | - una gomma bucata | *- oonah gohmah bookahtah*

My battery is flat | La mia batteria è scarica | *ah meeyah bahtehree yah eh skahrikah*
I don't have a spare tyre | Non ho una gomma di ricambio | *non oh oonah gohma dee reekambyoh*
I've run out of petrol | Ho finito la benzina | *oh feeneetoh lah behndzeenah*
My car doesn't start | La mia macchina non parte | *lah meeyah mahkeenah non parte*
Can you repair it? | La può aggiustare? | *lah pwoh ahjoostahreh?*
I have breakdown cover | Ho l'assicurazione contro i guasti | *oh lahseekoorahtsy ohneh kontroh ee gwahstee*

Problems with the authorities

I'm sorry, I didn't realise... | Mi dispiace, non sapevo che... | *mee deespyacheh, non sahpehvoh keh*
- I was driving so fast | - stavo guidando così veloce | *- stahvoh gweedah doh kohzee vehlohcheh*
- I went over the red lights | - sono passato/a con il semaforo rosso | *- oh sorpahsahtoh sehmahfohree rohsee*
- it was against the law | - era/fosse contro la legge | *- ehrah/fohsseh ko troh lah lehjeh*

Here are my documents | Ecco i miei documenti | *ehkoh ee myehee dohkoomehntee*
I'm innocent | Sono innocente | *sono eenohchente*

Dictionary

For those brave at heart, the English-Italian dictionary will help you build your own sentences. With the Italian-English one to interpret the replies, you can have a real conversation! The articles are listed with the nouns: **bambino/a**, **il/la** means that **il bambino** is a baby boy and **la bambina** a baby girl. It's the same for adjectives: **preferito/a** (favourite) indicates the masculine form is **preferito**, the feminine **preferita**. For the conjugation of verbs, here given in the infinitive "to do" form, see p.7 in the Introduction.

English-Italian dictionary

A

a(n)	un/una	oon/oonah
about (concerning)	al riguardo	ahl reegwardoh
accident	incidente, il	eencheedehnteh, eel
accommodation	alloggio, il	ahlohjoh, eel
A&E	pronto soccorso	prontoh sohkorsoh
aeroplane	aereo, il	ahehrehoh, eel
after	dopo	dohpoh
again	ancora	ahnkohrah
ago	fa	fah
airmail	posta aerea	pohstah ahehrehah
airport	aeroporto, il	ahehrohpohrtoh, eel
alarm	allarme, il	ahlarrneh, eel
all	tutto	tootoh
all right	apposto	ahpohstoh
allergy	allergia, la	ahlerjeeah, lah
ambulance	ambulanza, la	ahmboolahntsah, lah
America	America	ahmehreekah
American	americano/a	ahmehreekahnoh/ah
and	e	eh
another	un altro/un'altra	oon ahltroh/oonahltrah
to answer	rispondere	reespondehreh
any	qualsiasi	kwahlseeahsee
apartment	appartamento, il	ahpahrtahmehntoh, eel
appointment	appuntamento, il	ahpoontahmehntoh, eel
April	aprile	ahpreeleh
area	zona, la	dzohnah, lah
around	intorno	eentohrnoh
to arrange	arrangiare	ahrahnjahreh
arrival	arrivo	ahreevoh

art	**arte**	*ahrteh*

Some of the best places to check out Italian art – the
Uffizi in Florence, the Vatican Museum and the
Borghese Gallery in Rome.

to ask	chiedere	kyehdehreh
aspirin	aspirina, la	ahspeereenah, lah
at	a	ah
at home	a casa	ah cahzah
at last	alla fine	ahlah feeneh
at least	al meno	ahl mehnoh
at once	subito	soobeetoh
to attack	attaccare/aggredire	ahtahkahreh/ahgre-hdeereh
August	agosto	ahgohstoh
available	disponibile	deespohneebeeleh
away	via	veeah

baby	**bambino/a, il/la**	*bahmbeenoh/ah, eel/lah*
baggage	**bagaglio, il**	*bahgahlyoh, eel*
bar (pub)	**bar/pub**	*bar/pub*
bath	**bagno, il**	*bahnyoh, eel*
to be	**essere**	*ehsehreh*

beach   **la spiaggia**   *lah spyahjah*
You'll have to pay for your space on most beaches in
Northern Italy. Look for the **spiaggia libera**, which
allows free access to everyone.

because	**perché**	*pehrkeh*
before	**prima**	*preemah*
behind	**dietro**	*dyehtroh*
below	**sotto**	*sohtoh*
beside	**accanto a**	*ahkahntoh ah*
best	**migliore, il**	*meelyohreh, eel*
better	**meglio**	*mehlyoh*
between	**fra/tra**	*frah/trah*
bicycle	**bicicletta, la**	*beecheeklehtah, lah*
big	**grande**	*grahndeh*
bill	**conto, il**	*kohntoh, eel*
bit (a)	**pò, un**	*poh, oon*
boarding card	**carta d'imbarco, la**	*kartah deembahrkoh, lah*
book	**libro, il**	*leebroh, eel*
to book	**prenotare**	*prehnohtahreh*
booking	**prenotazione, la**	*prehnotahtsyohneh, lah*
box office	**botteghino, il**	*bohtehgheenoh, eel*
boy	**ragazzo, il**	*rahgahtsoh, eel*
brother	**fratello, il**	*frahtehloh, eel*
bureau de change	**ufficio cambio, il**	*oofeecho kahmbyoh, eel*
to burn	**bruciare**	*broochareh*
bus	**autobus, il**	*owtohboos, eel*
but	**ma**	*mah*
to buy	**comprare**	*komprahreh*
by (via)	**tramite**	*trahmeeteh*
by (beside)	**accanto**	*ahkahntoh*
by (by air, car)	**in in (in aereo/macchina)**	*een (een ahehrehoh/ mahkeenah)*

C

café	**caffè/bar, il**	*kahfeh/bar, eel*
to call	**chiamare**	*kyahmahreh*
camera	**macchina fotografi-ca, la**	*mahkeenah fohtohgrahfeekah, lah*
can (to be able)	**potere**	*pohtehreh*
to cancel	**annullare**	*ahnoolahreh*
car	**macchina, la**	*mahkeenah, lah*
cash	**contanti, i**	*kontahntee, ee*
cash point	**bancomat, il**	*bahnkohmat, eel*

cathedral	**la cattedrale**	*lah kahtehdrahleh*

The cathedral is the traditional centre of all Italian towns, and buildings are normally located in rings around this central piazza.

cd	**cd, il**	*cheedee, eel*
centre	**centro, il**	*chentroh, eel*
to change	**cambiare**	*kahmbyahreh*
charge (accusation)	**denuncia, la**	*dehnooncha, lah*
to charge	**far pagare**	*fahr pahgahreh*
cheap	**economico**	*ehkohnohmeekoh*
to check in (airport, hotel)	**check-in, fare, il**	*check-een, fahreh, eel*
cheque	**assegno, il**	*ahsehnyo, eel*
child	**bambino/a, il/la**	*bahmbeenoh/ah, eel/lah*
church	**chiesa, la**	*kyehsah, lah*
cinema	**cinema, il**	*cheenehmah, eel*
city	**città, la**	*cheetah, lah*
to close	**chiudere**	*kyoodehreh*
close by	**vicino**	*veecheenoh*
closed	**chiuso**	*kyoosoh*
clothes	**vestiti, i**	*vehsteetee, ee*
club	**discoteca, la**	*deeskohtehkah, lah*
coast	**costa, la**	*kohstah, lah*
cold	**freddo**	*frehdoh*
colour	**colore, il**	*kohlohreh, eel*
to come	**venire**	*vehneereh*
to complain	**lamentare**	*lahmehntahreh*
complaint	**reclamo, il**	*rehklahmoh, eel*
condom	**preservativo, il**	*prehzervateevoh, eel*
to confirm	**confermare**	*kohnfehrmahreh*
confirmation	**conferma, la**	*kohnfehrmah, lah*
congratulations!	**congratulazioni!/ auguri!**	*kohngrahtoolahtsyohnee!/owgooree!*
consulate	**consolato, il**	*kohnsohlahtoh, eel*
to contact	**contattare**	*kohntahtahreh*
contact lenses	**lenti a contatto, i**	*lehntee ah kontahtoh, ee*
contagious	**contagioso**	*kohntahjohzoh*
cool	**fresco**	*frehskoh*
cost	**costo, il**	*kostoh, eel*
to cost	**costare**	*kohstahreh*
cot	**culla, la**	*koolah, lah*
country	**paese, il**	*pahehzeh, eel*
countryside	**campagna, la**	*kahmpahnyah, lah*

credit card	**la carta di credito**	*lah kahrtah dee krehdeetoh*

Toll stations accept credit cards – skip the traffic and slide into the lanes marked Viacard.

crime	delitto, il	dehleetoh, eel
currency	valuta, la	vahlootah, lah
customer	cliente, il	kleeyehnteh, eel
customs	dogana, la	dohgahnah, lah
cut	taglio, il	tahlyoh, eel
to cut	tagliare	tahlyahreh
cycling	ciclismo, il	cheekleezmoh, eel

D

damage	danno, il	dahnoh, eel
danger	pericolo, il	pehreekohloh, eel
date (calendar)	data, la	dahtah, lah
daughter	figlia, la	feelyah, lah
day	giorno, il	johrnoh, eel
December	dicembre	deechembreh
to dehydrate	disidratarsi	deeseedrahtahrsee
delay	ritardo, il	reetahrdoh, eel
to dial	comporre il numero	kompohreh eel noomehroh
difficult	difficile	deefeecheeleh
directions	direzioni, le	deerehtsyohnee, leh
dirty	sporco/a	sporkoh/ah
disable	disabilitare	deezahbeeleetahreh
discount	sconto, lo	skohntoh, loh
disinfectant	disinfettante, il	deeseenfehtahnteh, eel
to disturb	disturbare	deestoorbahreh
doctor	dottore, il	dohtohreh/ mehdeekoh, eel
double	doppio	dohpyoh
down	giù	joo
to drive	guidare	gweedahreh
driver	austista, la	owteestah, lah
driving licence	patente, la	pahtenteh, lah
drug	droga, la	drohgah, lah
to dry-clean	lavare a secco	lahvahreh ah sehkoh
dry-cleaner's	tintoria, la	teentohreeah, lah
during	mentre	mehntreh
duty (tax)	dazio, il	dahtsyoh, eel

E

early	presto	prehstoh
to eat	mangiare	mahnjahreh
embassy	ambasciata, la	ahmbahshahtah, lah
emergency	emergenza, la	ehmehrjehntsah, lah
to enjoy	godere	gohdehreh
enough	abbastanza	ahbahstahntsah
error	errore, il	ehrohreh, eel
exactly	esattamente	ehzahtahmehnteh
exchange rate	tasso di cambio	tahsoh dee kahmbyoh
exhibition	mostra, la	mohstrah, lah
to export	esportare	espohtahreh
express (delivery, train)	espresso	ehsprehsoh

F

facilities	attrezzature, le	*ahtrehtsahtooreh, leh*
far	lontano	*lohntahno*
fast	veloce	*vehlohche*
father	padre	*pahdreh*
favourite	preferito/a	*prehfehreetoh/ah*
to fax	inviare un fax	*eenveeyahreh oon fax*
February	febbraio	*fehbrahyoh*
filling (station)	distributore di benz-ina	*deestreebootohreh dee behndzeenah*
film (camera)	pellicola, la	*pehleekohlah, lah*
film (cinema)	film, il	*feelm, eel*
to finish	finire	*feeneereh*
fire	fuoco, il	*fwohkoh, eel*
fire exit	uscita di sicurezza, la	*oosheetah dee seekoorehtsah, lah*
first aid	pronto soccorso	*prontoh sohkorsoh*
fitting room	camerino, il	*kahmehreenoh, eel*
flight	volo, il	*vohloh, eel*
flu	influenza, la	*eenflooehntsah, lah*
food poisoning	intossicazione ali-mentare	*eentohseekahtsyohneh ahleemehntahreh*

football	**il calcio**	*eel kahlcho*

Many stadiums, like San Siro in Milan, offer guided tours for football-lovers.

for	per	*pehr*
form (document)	documento, il	*dohkoomehntoh, eel*
free (vacant)	libero/a	*leebehroh/ah*
free (money)	gratis	*grahtees*
friend	amico/a, il/la	*ahmeekoh/ah, eel/lah*
from	da	*dah*

G

gallery	galleria, la	*gahlehreeyah, lah*
gas	benzina, la	*behndzeenah, lah*
gents	uomini	*wohmeenee*
to get	prendere	*prehndehreh*
girl	ragazza, la	*rahgahtsah, lah*
to give	dare	*dahreh*
glasses	occhiali, gli	*ohkyahlee, lyee*
to go	andare	*ahndahreh*
good	buono/a	*bwohnoh/ah*
group	gruppo, il	*groopoh, eel*
guarantee	garanzia, la	*gahrahntseeyah, lah*
guide	guida, la	*gweedah, lah*

H

hair	capelli, i	*kahpehlee, ee*
half	metà, la	*mehtah, lah*
to have	avere	*ahvehreh*
heat	calore, il	*kahlohreh, eel*
help!	aiuto!	*ayootoh!*

to help	**aiutare**	*ahyootahreh*
here	**qui**	*kwee*
high	**alto/a**	*ahltoh/ah*
to hire (a car)	**noleggiare (una macchina)**	*nohlejahreh (oonah mahkeenah)*

holiday   **la vacanza**   *lah vahkahntsah*
Visit one of Italy's many spa towns, with natural **terme** (thermal baths) for a totally relaxing holiday.

holidays	**ferie, le**	*fehryeh, leh*
homosexual	**omosessuale**	*ohmohsehsooahleh*
horse riding	**equitazione, la**	*ehkweetahtsyohneh, lah*
hospital	**ospedale, il**	*ozpehdahleh, eel*
hot	**caldo**	*kahldoh*
how?	**come?**	*kohmeh?*
how big?	**quanto grande?**	*kwahntoh grahndeh?*
how far?	**quanto dista?**	*kwahntoh deestah?*
how long?	**quanto?**	*kwahntoh?*
how much?	**quanto?**	*kwahntoh?*
to be hungry	**avere fame**	*ahvehreh fahmeh*
hurry up!	**sbrigati!**	*sbreegahtee!*
to hurt	**fare male**	*fahreh mahleh*
husband	**marito**	*mahreetoh*

I

identity card	**carta d'identità, la**	*kahrtah deedehnteetah, lah*
ill	**malato/a**	*mahlahtoh/ah*
immediately	**immediatamente**	*eemehdyahtahmehnteh*
to import	**importare**	*eempohrtahreh*
important	**importante**	*eempohrtahnteh*
in	**in**	*een*
information	**informazione, la**	*eenfohrmahtsyohneh, lah*
inside	**dentro**	*dehntro*
insurance	**assicurazione, la**	*ahseekoorahtsyohneh, lah*
interesting	**interessante**	*eentehrehsahnteh*
international	**internazionale**	*eentehrnahtsyohnahleh*
Ireland	**Irlanda**	*eerlahndah*
Irish	**irlandese**	*eerlahndehzeh*
Italy	**Italia**	*eetahlyah*
Italian	**italiano/a**	*eetahlyahnoh/ah*
itinerary	**itinerario, il**	*eeteenehrahryoh, eel*

J

January	**gennaio**	*jehnahyoh*
jellyfish	**medusa, la**	*mehdoozah, lah*
jet ski	**jet ski**	*jet ski*
journey	**viaggio, il**	*vyahjoh, eel*
July	**luglio**	*loolyoh*
junction	**svincolo, lo**	*zveenkohloh, loh*

| June | giugno | *joonyoh* |
| just (only) | appena | *ahpehnah* |

K
to keep	tenere	*tehnehreh*
key	chiave, la	*kyahveh, lah*
key ring	portachiavi, il	*pohrtahkyahvee, eel*
keyboard	tastiera, la	*tahstyehrah, lah*
kid	giovane	*johvahneh*
to kill	uccidere	*oocheedehreh*
kind (nice)	gentile	*jehnteeleh*
kind (sort)	tipo, un	*teepoh, oon*
kiosk	chiosco, il	*kyohskoh, eel*
kiss	bacio	*bahchoh*
to kiss	baciare	*bahchahreh*
to know (knowledge)	sapere	*sahpehreh*
to know (person)	conoscere	*kohnohshehreh*

L
label	etichetta, la	*ehteekehtah, lah*
ladies' (toilets)	bagno delle donne, il	*bahnyoh dehleh dohneh, eel*
lady	signora	*seenyohrah*

| language | **la lingua** | *lah leengwah* |

The word **lingua** also means tongue in Italian!

last	ultimo/a, il/la	*oolteemoh/ah, eel/lah*
late (delayed)	in ritardo	*een reetahrdoh*
late (time)	tardi	*tahrdee*
launderette	lavanderia, la	*lahvandehreeah, lah*
lawyer	avvocato, il	*ahvohkahtoh, eel*
to leave	partire	*pahrteereh*
left	sinistra	*seeneestrah*
less	meno	*mehnoh*
letter	lettera, la	*lehtehrah, lah*
life jacket	giubbotto di salvataggio, il	*joobohtoh dee sahlvahtahjoh, eel*
lifeguard	bagnino, il	*bahnyeenoh, eel*
lift	ascensore, il	*ahshensohreh, eel*
to like	piacere	*pyahchehreh*
to listen to	ascoltare	*ahskoltahreh*
little (a little)	poco	*pohkoh*
local	del posto	*dehl pohstoh*
to look	guardare	*gwahrdahreh*
to lose	perdere	*pehrdehreh*
lost property	oggetti smarriti	*ohjehteeh zmahreetek*
luggage	bagaglio, il	*bahgahlyoh, eel*

M
madam	signora	*seenyohrah*
mail	posta, la	*pohstah, lah*
main	principale	*preencheepahleh*

to make	**fare**	*fahreh*
man	**uomo, il**	*wohmoh, eel*
manager	**direttore, il**	*deerehtohreh, eel*
many	**molti**	*mohltee*
map (city)	**pianta della città, la**	*pyahntah dehlah cheetah, lah*
map (road)	**carta stradale, la**	*cahrtah strahdahleh, lah*
March	**marzo**	*mahrtsoh*
market	**mercato, il**	*mehrkahtoh, il*
married	**sposato/a**	*spozahtoh/ah*
May	**maggio**	*mahjoh*
maybe	**forse**	*forseh*
mechanic	**mecchanico, il**	*mehkahneekoh, eel*
to meet	**incontrare**	*eenkohntrahreh*
meeting	**riunione, la**	*reehoonyohneh, lah*
message	**messaggio, il**	*mehsahjoh, eel*
midday	**mezzogiorno, il**	*mehdsohjohrnoh, eel*
midnight	**mezzanotte, la**	*mehdsahnohteh, lah*
minimum	**minimo, il**	*meeneemoh, eel*
minute	**minuto, il**	*meenootoh, eel*
to miss (a person)	**sentire la mancanza**	*senteereh lah mahnkahntsah*
to miss (a train)	**perdere**	*pehrdehreh*
missing	**mancante**	*mahnkahnteh*
mobile phone	**cellulare, il**	*cheloolahreh, eel*
moment	**momento, il**	*mohmehntoh, eel*
money	**soldi, i**	*sohldee, ee*
more	**più**	*pyoo*

mosquito	**la zanzara**	*lah tzantzahrah*

In the countryside and cities, mosquitos are a common disturbance during the summertime, so pack your repellant!

most	**maggior parte**	*mahjohr pahrteh*
mother	**madre**	*mahdreh*
much	**molto**	*mohltoh*
museum	**museo, il**	*moosehoh, eel*
musical (a)	**musical, il**	*myoozeekahl, eel*
must	**dovere**	*dohvehreh*
my	**mio/a**	*meeyoh/yah*

N

name	**nome, il**	*nohmeh, eel*
near	**vicino**	*veecheenoh*
necessary	**necessario/a**	*nehchesahryoh/lah*
to need	**avere bisogno**	*ahvehreh beezohnyoh*
never	**mai**	*mayee*
new	**nuovo/a**	*nwohvoh/vah*
news	**notizie, le**	*nohteetsyeh, leh*
newspaper	**quotidiano/giornale, il**	*kwohteedyahnoh/johrnaleh, eel*
next	**prossimo/a**	*prohseemoh/ah*
next to	**accanto a**	*ahkahntoh ah*

nice (people)	**gentile**	*jehnteeleh*

Being told that you are **simpatico/a** is one of the highest compliments in Italian – difficult to translate, it means a good-hearted, kind person.

nice (things)	**piacevole**	*pyahchehvohleh*
night	**notte, la**	*nohteh, lah*
nightclub	**discoteca, la**	*deeskohtehkah, lah*
north	**nord**	*nohrd*
note (money)	**banconota, la/ biglietto, il**	*bahnkohnotah, lah/beelyehtoh, eel*
nothing	**niente**	*nyehnteh*
November	**novembre**	*nohvehmbreh*
now	**adesso**	*ahdehsoh*
nowhere	**da nessuna parte**	*dah nehsoonah pahrteh*
nudist beach	**spiaggia nudista, la**	*spyahjah noodeestah, lah*
number	**numero, il**	*noomehroh, eel*

O

object	**oggetto, il**	*ohjehtoh, eel*
October	**ottobre**	*ohtohbreh*
off (food)	**marcio/a**	*mahrtshoh/ah*
off (switched)	**spento/a**	*spehntoh/ah*
office	**ufficio, il**	*oofeecho, eel*
OK	**va bene**	*vah behneh*
on	**acceso/a**	*ahchehzoh/ah*
once	**una volta**	*oonah vohltah*
open	**aperto**	*ahpehrtoh*
to open	**aprire**	*ahpreereh*
opposite (place)	**di fronte**	*dee frohnteh*
optician's	**ottico, il**	*ohteekoh, eel*
or	**o**	*oh*
to order	**ordinare**	*ohrdeenahreh*
other	**altro/a**	*ahltroh/ah*
out of order	**fuori servizio**	*fwohree sehrveetsyoh*
outdoor	**all'aperto/fuori**	*ahlahpehrtoh/fwohreeh*
overnight	**pernottamento**	*pehrnohtahmehntoh*
owner	**proprietario/a, il/la**	*prohpreeyehtahryoh/lah eel/lah*
oxygen	**ossigeno, la**	*ohseejehnoh, lah*

P

painkiller	**antidolorifico, il**	*ahnteedohloh- reefeekoh, eel*
pair	**paio, il**	*pahyoh, eel*
parents	**genitori, i**	*jehneetohree, ee*
park	**parco, il**	*pahrkoh, eel*
to park	**parcheggiare**	*pahrkehjahreh*
parking	**parcheggio**	*pahrkehjoh*
party	**festa, la**	*fehstah, lah*
passport	**passaporto, il**	*pahsahpohrtoh, eel*
to pay	**pagare**	*pahgahreh*
people	**gente, la**	*jehnteh, lah*

| person | **persona, la** | *pehrsohnah, lah* |
| phone | **telefono, il** | *tehlehfohnoh, eel* |

to phone **telefonare** *tehlehfohnahreh*
Most public telephones only take pre-paid cards, rather than change.

photo	**foto, la**	*fohtoh, lah*
phrase book	**frasario, il**	*frahsahreeyoh, eel*
place	**posto, il**	*pohstoh, eel*
platform	**binario, il**	*beenahryoh, eel*
police	**polizia, la**	*pohleetseeyah, lah*
port (drink)	**porto, il**	*pohrtoh, eel*
port (sea)	**porto, il**	*pohrtoh, eel*
possible	**possibile**	*pohseebeeleh*
post	**posta, la**	*pohstah, lah*
post office	**ufficio postale, il**	*oofeecho pohstahleh, eel*
to prefer	**preferire**	*prehfehreereh*
prescription	**ricetta, la**	*reechehtah, lah*
pretty	**bello/a**	*behloh/ah*
price	**prezzo, il**	*prehtsoh, eel*
private	**privato/a**	*preevahtoh/ah*
probably	**probabilmente**	*prohbahbeelmehnteh*
problem	**problema, il**	*prohblehmah, eel*
pub	**pub/bar, il**	*pub/bar, eel*
public transport	**mezzi pubblici, i**	*mehtsee poobleechee, ee*
to put	**mettere**	*mehtehreh*

Q

quarter	**quarto**	*kwartoh*
question	**domanda, la**	*dohmahndah, lah*
queue	**coda, la**	*kohdah, lah*
quick	**veloce**	*vehlohcheh*
quickly	**velocemente**	*vehlohchehmehnteh*
quiet	**silenzioso/a**	*seelehntsyohzoh/ah*

R

railway	**ferrovia, la**	*fehrohveeyah, la*
rain	**pioggia, la**	*pyohjah, lah*
rape	**violentare**	*vyohlehntahreh*
ready	**pronto/a**	*prontoh/ah*
receipt	**scontrino, lo**	*skontreenoh, loh*
to receive	**ricevere**	*reechehvehreh*
reception	**reception, la**	*reception, lah*
receptionist	**receptionist, la**	*receptionist, lah*
to recommend	**raccommandare**	*rahkohmahndahreh*
reduction	**riduzione, la**	*reedootsyohneh, lah*
refund	**rimborso, il**	*reembohrsoh, eel*
to refuse	**rifiutare**	*reefyootahreh*
to relax	**rilassare**	*reelahsahreh*
rent	**affitto**	*ahfeetoh*

| to rent | affittare | ahfeetahreh |
| to request | richiedere | reekyehdehreh |

| reservation | la prenotazione | lah prehnoh-tahtsyohneh |

Other than regional trains, seat reservations are necessary for all train journeys.

to reserve	prenotare	prehnohtahreh
retired	in pensione	een pehnzyohneh
rich	ricco/a	reekoh/ah
to ride	andare in/a	ahndahreh een/lah
right	destra	dehstra
to be right	avere ragione	ahvehreh rahjohneh
to ring	suonare	swohnahreh
road	strada/via, la	strahdah/veeyah, lah
to rob	rubare	roobahreh
room	stanza, la	stahnsah, lah
route	itinerario, il	itinehraryoh, lah
rude	maleducato/a	mahlehdookahtoh/ah
to run	correre	kohrehreh

S

sad	triste	treesteh
safe	sicuro/a	seekooroh/ah
sailing boat	barca a vela, la	bahrkah ah vehlah, lah
sanitary towels	assorbenti, gli	ahsorbenteeh, lyee
sauna	sauna, la	sownah, lah
sea	mare, il	mahreh, eel
seat	sedia, la	sehdyah, eel
sedative	sedativo, il	sehdahteevoh, eel
self-service	self-service	self-servees
to sell	vendere	vehndehreh
to send	spedire/mandare/ inviare	spehdeereh/mahn-dahreh/eenveeyahreh
sensible	sensato/giudizioso	sehnsahtoh/jooditsyohzoh
September	settembre	sehtehmbre
to serve	servire	sehrveereh
service	servizio, il	sehrveetsyoh, eel
shaving cream	crema da barba, la	krehmah dahbahrbah, lah
shop	negozio, il	nehgohtsyoh, eel
shop assistant	commesso/a, il/la	kohmehsoh/sah, eel/lah
shopping	fare shopping	fahreh shopping/fahreh delyee ahk-weestee
shopping centre	centro commer-ciale, il	chentroh kohmehrchaleh, eel
short	corto/a	kohrtoh/ah
short cut	scorciatoia, la	skohrchatohyah, lah
show	spettacolo, lo	spehtahkohloh, loh
to show	mostrare	mohstrahreh

shower	doccia, la	_dohcha, lah_
shut	chiuso	_kyoozoh_
sign	segno, il	_sehnyoh, eel_
to sign	firmare	_feermahreh_
signature	firma, la	_feermah, lah_
since	da	_dah_
sir	signore	_seenyohreh_
sister	sorella, la	_sohrehlah, lah_
ski	sci, lo	_shee, loh_
to sleep	dormire	_dohrmeereh_
sleeping pill	sonnifero, il	_sohneefehroh, eel_
slow	lento/a	_lehntoh/lah_
small	piccolo/a	_peekohloh/lah_

to smoke	**fumare**	_foomahreh_

As of January 2005, smoking is banned in almost all restaurants, bars and public places (indoors only).

soft	morbido/a	_mohrbeedoh/dah_
some	del/qualche	_dehl/kwahlkeh_
something	qualcosa	_kwahlkohzah_
son	figlio, il	_feelyoh, eel_
soon	presto	_prehstoh_
south	sud	_sood_
speed	velocità	_vehlohcheetah_
sport	sport, lo	_sport, loh_
stadium	stadio, lo	_stahdyoh, loh_
stamp	francobollo, il	_frahnkohbohloh, eel_
to start	cominciare	_kohmeenchahreh_
to start (car)	accendere	_ahchendehreh_
station	stazione, la	_stahtsyohneh, lah_
sterling pound	sterlina, la	_sterleenah, lah_
to stop	smettere	_smehtehreh_
straight	dritto	_dreetoh_
street	strada, la	_strahdah, lah_
suddenly	improvisamente	_eemprohveezahmehnteh_
suitcase	valigia, la	_vahleejah, lah_
sun	sole, il	_sohleh, eel_

sunglasses	**occhiali**	_ohkyahlee dah_
	da sole, gli	_sohleh, lyee_

Want to know which sunglasses are this year's trendiest? Check out what the **carabinieri** are wearing!

| swimming pool | piscina, la | _peesheenah, lah_ |
| symptom | sintomo, il | _seentohmoh, eel_ |

T

table	tavola, la	_tahvohloh, eel_
to take	prendere/portare	_prehndehreh/ pohrtahreh_
tall	alto/a	_ahltoh/ah_

tampons	**tamponi/assorbenti interni, i/gli**	*tampohnee/lah-sohrbehntee een-tehrnee, eeh/lyee*
tax	**tassa, la**	*tahsah, lah*
tax-free	**esente tasse/tax-free**	*ehsehnteh tahseh//taksfree*
taxi	**taxi, il**	*tahxee, eel*
telephone	**telefono, il**	*tehlehfohnoh, eel*
telephone box	**cabina telefonica, la**	*kahbeenah tehle-hfohneekah, lah*
television	**televisione, la**	*tehlehveezyohneh, lah*
terrace	**terrazzo, il**	*tehrahtsoh, eel*
that	**quello/a**	*kwehloh/ah*
theft	**furto, il**	*foortoh, eel*
then	**poi**	*poy*
there	**là**	*lah*
thing	**cosa, la**	*kohzah, lah*
to think	**pensare**	*pehnsahreh*
thirsty	**assetato/a**	*ahsehtahtoh/ah*
this	**questo/a**	*kwehstoh/ah*
through	**attraverso**	*ahtrahvehrsoh*
ticket (bus, cinema)	**biglietto, il**	*beelyehtoh, eel*
ticket (parking)	**multa, la**	*mooltah, lah*
ticket office	**biglietteria, la**	*beelyehtehreeyah, lah*
time	**tempo, il**	*tehmpoh, eel*
time (clock)	**ora, la**	*ohrah, lah*
timetable	**orario, il**	*ohrahryoh, eel*
tip (money)	**mancia, la**	*mahnchah, lah*
tired	**stanco/a**	*stahnkoh/ah*
to	**a**	*ah*
today	**oggi**	*ohjee*
toilet	**gabinetto/bagno, il**	*gahbeenehtoh/bahny-oh, eel*
toiletries	**articoli da toilette**	*ahrteekohlee dah twahleht*
toll	**pedaggio, il**	*pehdahjoh, eel*
tomorrow	**domani**	*domahnee*
tonight	**stasera**	*stahsehrah*
too	**anche**	*ahnkeh*
tourist office	**ufficio di turismo, il**	*oofeecho dee tooreezmoh, eel*
town	**paese, il**	*pahehzeh, eel*
train	**treno, il**	*trehnoh, eel*

| tram | **il tram** | *eel tram* |

Stamp bus and tram tickets once you get on the transport itself.

to translate	**tradurre**	*trahdooreh*
travel	**viaggiare**	*vyahjahreh*
travel agency	**agenzia di viaggio, la**	*ahjehntseeyah dee vyahjoh, lah*
true	**vero/a**	*vehroh/ah*
typical	**tipico/a**	*teepeekoh/ah*

U

ugly	brutto/a	_broo_toh/ah
umbrella	ombrello, il	ohm_breh_loh, eel
uncomfortable	scomodo/a	_skoh_mohdoh/ah
unconscious (passed out)	perdere conoscenza	_pehr_dehreh kono_shent_sah
under	sotto	_soh_toh
to understand	capire	kah_pee_reh
up	su	soo
upstairs	al piano di sopra	ahl _pyah_noh dee _soh_prah
urgent	urgente	oor_jehn_teh
to use	usare	oo_sah_reh
useful	utile	_oo_teeleh
usually	di solito	dee _soh_leetoh

V

vacant	non occupato	non ohkoo_pah_toh
vacation	vacanza, la	vah_kahn_tsah, lah
vaccination	vaccinazione, la	vahcheenah_tsyoh_neh, lah
valid	valido	_vah_leedoh
value	valore, il	vah_loh_reh, eel
VAT	IVA	_ee_vah
vegetarian	vegetariano/a	vehjehtahr_yah_noh/ah
vehicle	veicolo, il	veh_ee_kohloh, eel
very	molto	_mohl_toh
visa	visto, il	_vee_stoh, eel
visit	visita, lah	_vee_zeetah, lah
to visit	visitare	veezee_tah_reh

W

waiter/waitress	cameriere/a, il/la	kahmehr_yeh_reh/ah, eel/lah
waiting room	sala d'attesa, la	_sah_lah dah_teh_zah, lah
to walk	camminare	kahmee_nah_reh
wallet	portafoglio, il	pohrtah_foh_lyoh, eel
to want	volere	voh_leh_reh
to wash	lavare	lah_vah_reh
watch	orologio, il	ohroh_loh_joh, eel
to watch	guardare	gwahr_dah_reh
water	acqua, la	_ah_kwah, lah
water sports	sport nautici, gli	sport _now_teechee, ee
way (manner)	modo, il	_moh_doh, lyee
way (route)	via, la	_vee_yah, lah
way in	entrata, la	ehn_trah_tah, lah
way out	uscita, la	oo_shee_tah, lah
weather	tempo, il	_tehm_poh, eel
web	tela, la	_teh_lah, lah
website	sito web, il	_see_toh web, eel
week	settimana, la	sehtee_mah_nah, lah
weekday (working day)	giorno feriale, il	_johr_noh fehr_yah_leh, eel
weekend	weekend/ fine settimana, il	weekend/_fee_nah sehtee_mah_nah, eel

welcome	benvenuto	behnveh<u>noo</u>toh
well	bene	<u>behneh</u>
west	ovest	<u>oh</u>vest
what?	cosa?	<u>koh</u>zah?
wheelchair	sedia a rotelle, la	<u>seh</u>dyah ah roh<u>teh</u>leh, lah
when?	quando?	<u>kwahn</u>doh?
where?	dove?	<u>doh</u>veh?
which?	quale?	<u>kwah</u>leh?
while	mentre	<u>mehn</u>treh
who?	chi?	kee?
why?	perché?	pehr<u>keh</u>?
wife	moglie	<u>moh</u>lyeh
with	con	kon
without	senza	<u>sehn</u>tsah
woman	donna, la	<u>doh</u>nah, lah
word	parola, la	pah<u>roh</u>lah, lah
work	lavoro, il	lah<u>voh</u>roh, il
to work (machine)	funzionare	foontsyoh<u>nah</u>reh
to work (person)	lavorare	lahvoh<u>rah</u>reh
world	mondo, il	<u>mohn</u>doh, eel
worried	preoccupato/a	prehohkoo<u>pah</u>toh/ah
worse	peggio	<u>peh</u>joh
to write	scrivere	<u>skree</u>vehreh
wrong (mistaken)	sbagliato/a	zbah<u>lyah</u>toh/ah

X

| x-ray | radiografia, la | rahdyohgrah<u>fee</u>yah, lah |

Y

year	anno, il	<u>ah</u>noh, eel
yearly	annuale	ahnoo<u>ah</u>leh
yes	sì	see
yesterday	ieri	<u>yeh</u>ree
young	giovane	<u>joh</u>vahneh

Z

| zoo | zoo, lo | tsoh, loh |

Italian-English dictionary

A

a	*ah*	at
a	*ah*	to
a casa	*ah cahzah*	at home
abbastanza	*ahbahstahntsah*	enough
accanto	*ahkahntoh*	by (beside)
accanto a	*ahkahntoh ah*	beside/next to
accendere	*ahchendehreh*	to start (car)
acceso/a	*ahchezoh/zah*	on
acqua, la	*ahkwah, lah*	water
adesso	*ahdehsoh*	now
aereo, il	*ahehrehoh, eel*	aeroplane
aeroporto, il	*ahehrohpohrtoh, eel*	airport
affari, gli	*ahfahree, lyee*	business
affittare	*ahfeetahreh*	to rent
affitto	*ahfeetoh*	rent
agenzia di viaggio, la	*ahjehntseeyah dee vyahjoh, lah*	travel agency
aggredire	*ahgrehdeereh*	to attack

agosto	*ahgohstoh*	**August**

Italy shuts down in August, with the exception of seaside towns. Head to the beach!

AIDS	*ayds*	AIDS
aiutare	*ahyootahreh*	to help
aiuto!	*ayootoh!*	help!
al meno	*ahl mehnoh*	at least
al piano di sopra	*ahl pyahnoh dee sohprah*	upstairs
al riguardo	*ahl reegwardoh*	about (concerning)
alarme antincendio, il	*ahlahrmeh ahnteechendyoh, eel*	fire alarm
all'aperto	*ahlahpehrtoh*	outdoor/outside
alla fine	*ahlah feeneh*	at last
allarme, il	*ahlahrmeh, eel*	alarm
allergia, la	*ahlerjeeah, lah*	allergy
alloggio, il	*ahlohjoh, eel*	accommodation
alto/a	*ahltoh/ah*	high/tall
altro/a	*ahltroh/ah*	other
ambasciata, la	*ahmbahshahtah, lah*	embassy
ambulanza, la	*ahmboolahntsah, lah*	ambulance
America	*ahmehreekah*	America
americano/a	*ahmehreekahnoh/ah*	American
amico/a, il/la	*ahmeekoh/ah, eel/lah*	friend
anche	*ahnkeh*	too
ancora	*ahnkohrah*	again/yet
andare	*ahndahreh*	to go
andare in/a	*ahndahreh een/ah*	to ride
anniversario, il	*ahneevehrsahreeoh, eel*	anniversary

anno, il	*ahnoh, eel*	year
annuale	*ahnooahleh*	yearly
annullare	*ahnoolahreh*	to cancel
antidolorifico, il	*ahnteedohlohree-feekoh, eel*	painkiller
aperto	*ahpehrtoh*	open
appartamento, il	*ahpahrtahmehntoh, eel*	apartment
appena	*ahpehnah*	just (only)
apposto	*ahpohstoh*	all right
appuntamento, il	*ahpoontahmehntoh, eel*	appointment
aprile	*ahpreeleh*	April
aprire	*ahpreereh*	to open
arrangiare	*ahrahnjiahreh*	to arrange
arredata	*ahrehdahtah*	furnished
arrivo	*ahreevoh*	arrival
arte	*ahrteh*	art
articoli da toilette	*ahrteekohlee dah twahleht*	toiletries
ascensore, il	*ahshensohreh, eel*	lift
ascoltare	*ahskoltahreh*	to listen to
aspirina, la	*ahspeereenah, lah*	aspirin

| **il assegno** | *eel ahsehnyoh* | cheque |

Unless you have an Italian account, don't even think about trying to pay with a cheque – they are rarely (if ever) accepted.

assetato/a	*ahsehtahtoh/ah*	thirsty
assicurazione, la	*ahseekoorah-tsyohneh, lah*	insurance
assorbenti, gli	*ahsorbenteeh, lyee*	sanitary towels
assorbenti interni, gli	*ahsohrbehntee een-tehrnee, lyee*	tampons
attaccare	*ahtahkahreh*	to attack
attenzione	*ahtehntsyoneh*	attention
attraverso	*ahtrahvehrsoh*	through
attrezzature, le	*ahtrehtsahtooreh, leh*	facilities
autista, la	*owteestah, lah*	driver
Australia	*owstrahlyah*	Australia
australiano/a	*owstrahlyahnoh/ah*	Australian
autobus, il	*owtohboos, eel*	bus
avere	*ahvehreh*	to have
avere bisogno	*ahvehreh beezohnyoh*	to need
avere fame	*ahvehreh fahmeh*	to be hungry
avere ragione	*ahvehreh rahjohneh*	to be right
avvocato, il	*ahvohkahtoh, eel*	lawyer

B

baciare	*bahchyahreh*	to kiss
bacio	*bahcho*	kiss
bagaglio, il	*bahgahlyoh, eel*	baggage
bagnino, il	*bahnyeenoh, eel*	lifeguard
bagno, il	*bahnyoh, eel*	bath/toilet

bagno delle donne, il	*bahnyoh dehleh dohneh, eel*	ladies' (toilets)
bambino/a, il/la	*bahmbeenoh/ah, eel/lah*	baby/child
bancomat, il	*bahnkohmat, eel*	cash point
banconota, il	*bankohnohtah, eel*	note (money)
bar/pub	*bar/pub*	bar (pub)
barca a vela, la	*bahrkah ah vehlah, lah*	sailing boat
bello/a	*behloh/ah*	pretty
ben fatto/ complimenti	*behn fahtoh/ kompleemehntee*	well done
bene	*behneh*	well
benvenuto	*behnvehnootoh*	welcome
benzina, la	*behntseenah, lah*	gas
biancheria intima, la	*byahnkehreeyah eenteemah, lah*	underwear
biblioteca, la	*beebleeohtehkah, lah*	library
bicicletta, la	*beecheeklehtah, lah*	bicycle
biglietteria, la	*beelyehtehreeyah, lah*	ticket office

il biglieto	*eel beelyehtoh*	ticket (bus/train/ cinema)

Make sure to stamp your train ticket with the date
(look for the yellow boxes in the station) before boarding,
in order to avoid a fine.

binario, il	*beenahreeyoh, eel*	platform
botteghino, il	*bohtehgheenoh, eel*	box office
box/posto-macchina, il	*box/postoh-mahkeenah, eel*	garage
bruciare	*broochahreh*	to burn
brutto/a	*brootoh/ah*	ugly
buono/a	*bwohnoh/ah*	good
business	*beezness*	business class
bussare	*boosahreh*	to knock

C

cabina telefonica, la	*kahbeenah tehlehfohneekah, lah*	telephone box
caffè/bar, il	*kahfeh/bar, eel*	café
calcio, il	*kahlcho, eel*	football
calcolatrice, la	*kahlkohlahtreecheh, lah*	calculator
caldo	*kahldoh*	hot
calore, il	*kahlohreh, eel*	heat
cambiare	*kahmbyahreh*	to change
cameriere/a, il/la	*kahmehryehreh/ah, eel/lah*	waiter/waitress
camerino, il	*kahmehreenoh, eel*	fitting room
camminare	*kahmeenahreh*	to walk
campagna, la	*kahmpahnyah, lah*	countryside
campo da tennis, il	*kahmpoh da tehnees, eel*	tennis court
campo di golf, il	*kahmpoh dee golf, eel*	golf course

capelli, i	kah*pehlee*, ee	hair
capire	kah*peereh*	to understand
carabinieri, i	kahrahbeen*yehree*, ee	police (Italian military branch)
carta d'identità, la	<u>kah</u>rtah deedehntee-<u>tah</u>, lah	identity card
carta d'imbarco, la	kartah deem<u>bahr</u>koh, lah	boarding card
carta da lettere, la	<u>kah</u>rtah dah <u>leh</u>tehreh, lah	writing paper
carta di credito, la	<u>kah</u>rtah dee <u>kreh</u>dee-toh, lah	credit card
cartina, la	kahr<u>tee</u>nah, lah	cigarette paper
cartoleria, la	kahrtohleh<u>ree</u>yah, lah	stationer's
casinò, il	kahzee<u>noh</u>, eel	casino
cattedrale, la	kahteh<u>drah</u>leh, lah	cathedral
cd, il	<u>chee</u>dee, eel	cd
cellulare, il	cheloo<u>lah</u>reh, eel	mobile phone
centro, il	<u>chen</u>troh, eel	centre
centro commerciale, il	<u>chen</u>troh kohmehr<u>cha</u>leh, eel	shopping centre
cerniera, la	chern<u>yeh</u>rah, lah	zip
check-in, fare il	check-een, fareh eel	to check in (airport/hotel)
chi?	kee?	who?
chiamare	kyah<u>mah</u>reh	to call
chiave, la	<u>kyah</u>veh, lah	key
chiedere	<u>kyeh</u>dehreh	to ask
chiesa, la	<u>kyeh</u>sah, lah	church
chiosco, il	<u>kyoh</u>skoh, eel	kiosk
chiudere	<u>kyoo</u>dehreh	to close
chiuso	<u>kyoo</u>soh	closed/shut
ci vediamo dopo	chee veh<u>dyah</u>moh <u>doh</u>poh	see you later
ciclismo, il	chee<u>kleez</u>moh, eel	cycling
cinema, il	<u>chee</u>nehmah, eel	cinema
cintura di sicurezza, la	cheen<u>too</u>rah dee seekoo<u>reh</u>tsah, lah	seat belt
città, la	chee<u>tah</u>, lah	city
cliente, il	klee<u>ehn</u>teh, eel	customer
coda, la	<u>koh</u>dah, lah	queue
cognome, il	koh<u>nyoh</u>meh, eel	surname
colore, il	koh<u>loh</u>reh, eel	colour
come?	<u>koh</u>meh?	how?
cominciare	kohmeen<u>chah</u>reh	to start
commesso/a, il/la	koh<u>meh</u>soh/ah, eel/lah	shop assistant
comporre il numero	kom<u>poh</u>reh eel <u>noo</u>mehroh	to dial
comprare	kom<u>prah</u>reh	to buy
con	kon	with
conferma, la	kohn<u>fehr</u>mah, lah	confirmation
confermare	kohnfehr<u>mah</u>reh	to confirm
congratulazioni!/ auguri!	kohngrahtoolah<u>tsyoh</u>nee!/owg<u>oo</u>ree!	congratulations!
conoscere	koh<u>noh</u>shereh	to know (person)

| consigliare | konseelyahreh | to recommend |

il consolato   *il kohnsohlahtoh*   consulate
Take a minute to check the location of the nearest consulate to where you are travelling – most are in Milan or Rome.

contagioso	kohntahjohzoh	contagious
contanti, i	kontahntee, ee	cash
contattare	kohntahtahreh	to contact
conto, il	kohntoh, eel	bill
correre	kohrehreh	to run
corto/a	kohrtoh/ah	short
cosa?	kohzah?	what?
cosa, la	kohzah, lah	thing
costa, la	kohstah, lah	coast
costare	kohstahreh	to cost
costo, il	kostoh, eel	cost
crema, la	krehmah, lah	cream
crema da barba, la	krehmah dee bahrbah, lah	shaving cream
crema doposole, la	krehmah doh-pohsohleh, lah	after sun-lotion
cuffia, la	koofyah, lah	bathing cap
culla, la	koolah, lah	cot

D

da	dah	from/since
da nessuna parte	dah nehsoonah pahrteh	nowhere
danno, il	dahnoh, eel	damage
dare	dahreh	to give
data, la	dahtah, lah	date (calendar)
dazio, il	dahtsyoh, eel	duty (tax)
del	dehl	some
del posto	dehl postoh	local
delitto, il	dehleetoh, eel	crime
dentro	dehntro	inside
denuncia, la	dehnooncha, lah	charge (accusation)
destra	dehstra	right
di fronte	dee frohnteh	opposite (place)
di solito	dee sohleetoh	usually
dicembre	deechembreh	December
dietro	dyehtroh	behind
difficile	deefeecheeleh	difficult
dipendenti, i	deepehndehntee, ee	staff
direttore, il	deerehtohreh, eel	manager
direzioni, le	deerehtsyohnee, leh	directions
disabilitare	deezahbeeleetahreh	disable

la discoteca   *lah deeskohtehkah*   club/disco/nightclub
If you love to dance, head over to the Adriatic coast near Rimini, known for its summer club scene.

disidratarsi	*deeseedrah<u>tahr</u>see*	to dehydrate
disinfettante, il	*deeseenfeh<u>tahn</u>teh, eel*	disinfectant
disoccupato/a	*deezohkoo<u>pah</u>toh/ah*	unemployed
disponibile	*deespohnee<u>bee</u>leh*	available
distributore di benzina	*deestreeboo<u>toh</u>reh dee behn<u>tsee</u>nah*	filling (station)
disturbare	*deestoor<u>bah</u>reh*	to disturb
doccia, la	*<u>doh</u>cha, lah*	shower
documento, il	*dohkoo<u>mehn</u>toh, eel*	form (document)
dogana, la	*doh<u>gah</u>nah, lah*	customs
domanda, la	*doh<u>mahn</u>dah, lah*	question
domani	*doh<u>mah</u>nee*	tomorrow
donna, la	*<u>doh</u>nah, lah*	woman
dopo	*<u>doh</u>poh*	after
doppio	*<u>doh</u>pyoh*	double
dormire	*dohr<u>mee</u>reh*	to sleep
dottore	*doh<u>toh</u>reh*	doctor
dove?	*<u>doh</u>veh?*	where?
dovere	*doh<u>veh</u>reh*	must
dritto	*<u>dree</u>toh*	straight
droga, la	*<u>droh</u>gah, lah*	drug
droghe, le	*<u>droh</u>geh, leh*	drugs

E

e	*eh*	and
economico	*ehkoh<u>noh</u>meekoh*	cheap
e-mail	*e-mail*	e-mail
emergenza, la	*ehmehr<u>jehn</u>tsah, lah*	emergency
entrata, la	*ehn<u>trah</u>tah, lah*	way in
equitazione, la	*ehkweetaht<u>syoh</u>neh, lah*	horse riding
errore, il	*eh<u>rohr</u>eh, eel*	error
esattamente	*ehzahtah<u>mehn</u>teh*	exactly
esente tasse	*ehsen<u>teh</u> <u>tah</u>seh*	tax-free
esportare	*espohr<u>tah</u>reh*	to export
espresso	*eh<u>spreh</u>soh*	express (delivery/train)
essere	*eh<u>seh</u>reh*	to be
ettichetta, la	*ehtee<u>keh</u>tah, lah*	label

F

fa	*fah*	ago
far pagare	*fahr pah<u>gah</u>reh*	to charge
fare	*<u>fah</u>reh*	to make
fare degli acquisti	*<u>fah</u>reh <u>del</u>yee akwee<u>stee</u>*	shopping
fare lo spelling	*<u>fah</u>reh loh <u>speh</u>leeng*	to spell
fare male	*<u>fah</u>reh <u>mah</u>leh*	to hurt
fare una domanda	*<u>fah</u>reh oonah doh<u>mahn</u>dah*	query
fare una radiografia	*<u>fah</u>reh oonah radio<u>grafia</u>*	to x-ray
febbraio	*feh<u>brah</u>yoh*	February
ferie, le	*<u>feh</u>reeyeh, leh*	holidays
fermata d'autobus, la	*fehr<u>mah</u>tah <u>dow</u>to-hbus, lah*	bus stop

ferrovia, la	*fehrohveeyah, lah*	railway
festa, la	*fehstah, lah*	party
figlia, la	*feelyah, lah*	daughter
figlio,il	*feelyoh, eel*	son
film, il	*feelm, eel*	film (cinema)

la fine settimana	*lah feenah sehteemahnah*	weekend

Typical Italian school hours are 8.30am-12.30pm, Monday through Saturday.

finire	*feeneereh*	to finish
firma, la	*feermah, lah*	signature
firmare	*feermahreh*	to sign
forse	*forseh*	maybe
foto, il	*fohtoh, eel*	photo
fra	*frah*	between
francobollo, il	*frahnkohbohloh, eel*	stamp
frasario, il	*frahsahreeyoh, eel*	phrase book
fratello, il	*frahtehloh, eel*	brother
freddo	*frehdoh*	cold
fresco	*frehskoh*	cool
fumare	*foomahreh*	to smoke
funzionare	*foontsyohnahreh*	to work (machine)
fuoco, il	*fwohkoh, eel*	fire
fuori servizio	*fwohree sehrveetsyoh*	out of order
furto, il	*foortoh, eel*	theft

gabinetto	*gahbeenehtoh*	toilet
galleria, la	*gahlehreeyah, lah*	gallery
Galles	*gahles*	Wales
gallese	*gahlehzeh*	Welsh
garanzia, la	*gahrahntseeyah, lah*	guarantee
genitori, i	*jehneetohree, ee*	parents
gennaio	*jehnahyoh*	January
gente, la	*jehnteh, lah*	people
gentile	*jehnteeleh*	kind/nice

il giornale	*eel johrnaleh*	newspaper

All major newspapers in Italy are associated with a specific city, where they are printed and primarily distributed.

giorno, il	*johrnoh, eel*	day
giorno feriale, il	*johrnoh fehryahleh, eel*	weekday (working day)
giovane	*johvahneh*	young
giù	*joo*	down
giubbotto di salvataggio, il	*jewbohtoh dee sahlvahtahjoh, eel*	life jacket
giudizioso	*joodeetsyohzoh*	sensible
giugno	*joonyoh*	June
godere	*gohdehreh*	to enjoy
golf	*golf*	golf

grande	*grahndeh*	big
gratis	*grahtees*	free (money)
gruppo, il	*groopoh, eel*	group
guardare	*gwahrdahreh*	to look/to watch
guida, la	*gweedah, lah*	guide
guidare	*gweedahreh*	to drive

I

ieri	*yehree*	yesterday
immediatamente	*eemehdeeyahtah-mehnteh*	immediately
impiegare qualcuno	*eempyehgahreh kwalkoono*	to hire someone
importante	*eempohrtahnteh*	important
importare	*eempohrtahreh*	to import
improvisamente	*eemprohveezahmehnteh*	suddenly
in	*een*	in
in (in aereo/ macchina)	*een (een aehreoh/ mahkeenah)*	by (by air, car)
in pensione	*een pehnzyohneh*	retired
in ritardo	*een reetahrdoh*	late (delayed)
incidente, il	*eencheedehnteh, eel*	accident
incontrare	*eenkohntrahreh*	to meet
influenza, la	*eenflooehntsah, lah*	flu
informazione, la	*eenfohrmahtsyohneh, lah*	information
Inghilterra	*eengeeltehrah*	England
inglese	*eenglehseh*	English
interessante	*eentehrrehsahnteh*	interesting
internazionale	*eentehrnahtsy-ohnahleh*	international
intorno	*eentohrnoh*	around
intossicazione alimentare	*eentohseekahtsyohneh ahleemehntahreh*	food poisoning
inviare	*eenveeyahreh*	to send
inviare un fax	*eenveeyahreh oon fax*	to fax
Irlanda	*eerlahndah*	Ireland
irlandese	*eerlahndehseh*	Irish
isola, la	*eezohlah, lah*	island
Italia	*eetahlyah*	Italy
italiano/a	*eetahlyahnoh/ah*	Italian
itinerario, il	*eeteenehrahryoh, eel*	itinerary/route
IVA	*eevah*	VAT

J

| jet ski | *jet ski* | jet-ski |

L

là	*lah*	there
lamentare	*lahmehntahreh*	to complain
lametta, la	*lahmehtah, lah*	razor blade
lavanderia, la	*lahvahndehreeyah, lah*	launderette
lavare	*lahvahreh*	to wash
lavare a secco	*lahvahreh ah sehkoh*	to dry clean
lavorare	*lahvohrahreh*	to work (person)

| avoro, il | lahvohroh, eel | work |

| **lei** | *lay* | **you (formal)** |

Use the formal 'lei' in business, and when speaking
with anyone older than yourself.

enti a contatto, i	lehntee ah kontahtoh, ee	contact lenses
ento/a	lehntoh/ah	slow
ettera, la	lehtehra, lah	letter
ibero/a	leebehroh/ah	free (vacant)
ibro, il	leebroh, eel	book
ingua, la	leengwah, lah	language
ontano	lohntahno	far
uglio	loolyoh	July

M

na	mah	but
nacchia, la	mahkyah, lah	stain
nacchina, la	mahkeenah, lah	car
nacchina fotografica, la	mahkeenah fohto-hgrahfeekah, lah	camera
nadre	mahdreh	mother
nagari	mahgahree	perhaps
naggio	mahjoh	May
naggior parte	mahjohr pahrteh	most
nai	mayee	never
nalato/a	mahlahtoh/ah	ill
naleducato/a	mahlehdookahtoh/ah	rude
nancante	mahnkahnteh	missing
nancanza, la	mahnkahntsah, la	shortage
nancia, la	mahncha, lah	tip (money)
nandare	mahndahreh	to send
nandare un messaggio/sms	mahndahreh oon mehsahjoh/sms	to send a text message
nangiare	mahnjahreh	to eat
narcio/a	mahrtshoh/ah	off (food)
nare, il	mahreh, eel	sea
narito	mahreetoh	husband
narzo	mahrtsoh	March
necchanico, il	mehkahneekoh, eel	mechanic
nedico, il	medeekoh, eel	doctor

| **la medusa** | *lah mehdoozah* | **jellyfish** |

Be careful in summer, as jellyfish are a common sight
off the coasts of Italy.

eglio	mehlyoh	better
eno	mehnoh	less
entre	mehntreh	during/while
eraviglioso	mehrahveelyohzoh	wonderful
ercato, il	mehrkahtoh, il	market
essaggio, il	mehsahjoh, eel	message

metà, la	*meh<u>tah</u>, lah*	half
metropolitana, la	*mehtrohpohlee-tah<u>nah</u>, lah*	underground (tube)
mettere	*<u>meh</u>tehreh*	to put
mezzanotte, la	*mehtsah<u>noh</u>teh, lah*	midnight
mezzi pubblici, i	*<u>meh</u>tsee poo<u>blee</u>chee, ee*	public transport
mezzogiorno, il	*mehtsoh<u>joh</u>rnoh, eel*	midday
migliore, il	*mee<u>lyoh</u>reh, eel*	best
minimo, il	*<u>mee</u>neemoh, eel*	minimum
minuto, il	*mee<u>noo</u>toh, eel*	minute
mio/a	*<u>mee</u>yoh/ah*	my
modo, il	*<u>moh</u>doh, eel*	way (manner)
moglie	*<u>moh</u>lyeh*	wife
molti	*<u>moh</u>ltee*	many
molto	*<u>moh</u>ltoh*	much/very
momento, il	*moh<u>meh</u>ntoh, eel*	moment
mondo, il	*<u>moh</u>ndoh, eel*	world
morbido/a	*<u>moh</u>rbeedoh/ah*	soft
mostra, la	*<u>moh</u>strah, lah*	exhibition
mostrare	*moh<u>strah</u>reh*	to show
multa, la	*<u>moo</u>ltah, lah*	ticket (parking)
municipio, il	*moonee<u>chee</u>pyoh, eel*	town hall
museo, il	*moo<u>seh</u>oh, eel*	museum
musical, il	*myoozee<u>kah</u>l, eel*	musical (a)
mutande, le	*moo<u>tah</u>ndeh, leh*	underwear

N

nazionalità, la	*nahtsyohnahlee<u>tah</u>, lah*	nationality
necessario/a	*nehche<u>sah</u>ryoh/ah*	necessary
negozio, il	*neh<u>goh</u>tsyoh, eel*	shop
niente	*<u>nyeh</u>nteh*	nothing
noleggiare una macchina	*nohle<u>jah</u>reh <u>oo</u>nah <u>mah</u>keenah*	to hire a car
nome, il	*<u>noh</u>meh, eel*	name
non occupato	*non ohkoo<u>pah</u>toh*	vacant
nord	*nohrd*	north
notizie, le	*noh<u>tee</u>tsyeh, leh*	news
notte, la	*<u>noh</u>teh, lah*	night
novembre	*noh<u>veh</u>mbreh*	November
numero, il	*<u>noo</u>mehroh, eel*	number
nuovo/a	*<u>nwoh</u>voh/ah*	new

O

o	*oh*	or
occhiali, gli	*oh<u>kyah</u>lee, lyee*	glasses
occhiali da sole, gli	*oh<u>kyah</u>lee dah <u>soh</u>leh, lyee*	sunglasses
oggetti preziosi/di valore, gli	*oh<u>jeh</u>tee pret<u>syoh</u>zee/dee vah<u>loh</u>reh, lyee*	valuables
oggetti smarriti	*oh<u>jeh</u>tee zmah<u>ree</u>teh*	lost property
oggetto, il	*oh<u>jeh</u>toh, eel*	object
oggi	*<u>oh</u>jee*	today

il ombrello *eel ohmbrehloh* umbrella
On average, Italy's wettest month is November, so don't forget your umbrella.

omosessuale	ohmohsehsooahleh	homosexual
operatrice, la	ohpehrahtreecheh, lah	operator
ora, la	ohrah, lah	time (clock)
orario, il	ohrahreeyoh, eel	timetable
ordinare	ohrdeenahreh	to order
orologio, il	ohrohlohjoh, eel	watch
ospedale, il	ozpehdahleh, eel	hospital
ossigeno, la	ohseejahnoh, lah	oxygen
ostello della gioventù, il	ohstehloh dehlah johvehntoo, eel	youth hostel
ottico, il	ohteekoh, eel	optician's
ottobre	ohtohbreh	October
ovest	ohvest	west
padre	pahdreh	father
paese, il	pahyehzeh, eel	country/town
pagare	pahgahreh	to pay
pagine gialle, le	pahjeeneh jahleh, leh	yellow pages
paio, il	pahyoh, eel	pair
parcheggiare	pahrkehjahreh	to park
parcheggio	pahrkehjoh	parking
parco, il	pahrkoh, eel	park
parola, la	pahrohlah, lah	word
parrucchiere, il	pahrookyehreh, eel	hairdresser's
partire	pahrteereh	to leave
passaporto, il	pahsahpohrtoh, eel	passport
passare di stomaco	pahsahreh dee stohmakoh	to vomit
patente, la	pahtenteh, lah	driving licence
pedaggio, il	pehdahjoh, eel	toll
peggio	pehjoh	worse
pellicola, la	pehleekohlah, lah	film (camera)

penottamento *pehrnohtahmehntoh* overnight
Travel in style – cappuccino included! – on one of the many overnight trains that run between northern and southern Italy.

pensare	pehnsahreh	to think
per	pehr	for
perché	pehrkeh	because
perché?	pehrkeh?	why?
perdere	pehrdehreh	to lose/to miss (a train)
perdere conoscenza	perdereh konoshentsah	unconscious (passed out)
pericolo, il	pehreekohloh, eel	danger
persona, la	pehrsohnah, lah	person

Italian	Pronunciation	English
piacere	*pyahchehreh*	to like
piacevole	*pyahchevohleh*	nice (things)
pianta della città, la	*pyahnta dehlah cheetah, lah*	map (city)
pianta stradale, la	*pyahnta strahdahleh, lah*	map (road)
piazza	*pyahtsah*	square (place)
piccolo/a	*peekohloh/lah*	small
pioggia, la	*pyohjah, lah*	rain
piscina, la	*peesheenah, lah*	swimming pool
più	*pyoo*	more
piuttosto	*pyootohstoh*	quite
pò, un	*poh, oon*	bit (a)
poco	*pohkoh*	little (a little)
poi	*poy*	then
polizia, la	*pohleetseeyah, lah*	police
portachiavi, il	*pohrtahkyahvee, eel*	key ring
portafoglio, il	*pohrtahfohlyoh, eel*	wallet
portare	*pohrtahreh*	to take/to bring
porto, il	*pohrtoh, eel*	port (drink, sea)
possibile	*pohseebeeleh*	possible
posta, la	*pohstah, lah*	mail
posta aerea	*pohstah ahehrehah*	airmail
posta elettronica, la	*pohstah ehlehtrohneekah, lah*	e-mail
postazione taxi, la	*pohstahtsyohneh taxee, lah*	taxi rank
posto, il	*pohstoh, eel*	place
potere	*pohtehreh*	can (to be able)
preferire	*prehfehreereh*	to prefer
preferito/a	*prehfehreetoh/ah*	favourite
prefisso telefonico, il	*prehfeesoh tehlehfohneekoh, eel*	area code
prendere	*prehndehreh*	to get
prendere	*prehndehreh*	to take
prenotare	*prehnohtahreh*	to book
prenotazione, la	*prehnotahtsyohneh, lah*	booking
preoccupato/a	*prehohkoopahtoh/ah*	worried
preservativo, il	*prehzervateevoh, eel*	condom
presto	*prehstoh*	early
prezzo, il	*prehtsoh, eel*	price
prima	*preemah*	before
principale	*preencheepahleh*	main
privato/a	*preevahtoh/ah*	private
probabilmente	*prohbahbeelmehnteh*	probably
problema, il	*prohblchmah, cel*	problem
pronto/a	*prohntoh/ah*	ready
pronto soccorso	*prohntoh sokohrzoh*	A&E/first aid
proprietario/a, il/la	*prohpreeyehtahryeeoh/ah, eel/lah*	owner
prossimo/a	*prohseemoh/ah*	next
pub/bar, il	*pub/bar, eel*	pub
puntura di zanzara, la	*poontoorah dee tsantsahrah, lah*	mosquito bite

Q

qualcosa	*kwahlkohzah*	something
qualche	*kwahlkeh*	some
quale?	*kwahleh?*	which?
qualità, la	*kwahleetah, lah*	quality
qualsiasi	*kwalseeahsee*	any
quantità, la	*kwahndoh?*	when?
quando?	*kwahnteetah, lah*	quantity
quanto?	*kwahntoh?*	how long?/how much?
quanto dista?	*kwahntoh deeztah?*	how far?
quanto grande?	*kwahntoh grahndeh?*	how big?
quarto	*kwartoh*	quarter
quello/a	*kwehloh/lah*	that
questo/a	*kwehstoh/ah*	this
qui	*kwee*	here
quiz, il	*kweets, eel*	quiz
quotidiano, il	*kwohteedyahnoh, eel*	newspaper

R

raccommandare	*rahkohmehndahreh*	to recommend
radio, la	*rahdeeyoh, lah*	radio
radiografia, la	*rahdyohgrahfeeyah, lah*	x-ray
radiografie, le	*rahdiografeeyeh, leh*	x-rays
ragazza, la	*rahgahtsah, lah*	girl

il ragazzo	*il rahgahtsoh*	**boy**

Ragazzo/a is also the informal way to refer to your boyfriend or girlfriend.

ragnatela, la	*ranyahtehlah, lah*	spider web
reception, la	*reception/lah*	reception
receptionist, la	*receptionist, lah*	receptionist
reclamo, il	*rehklahmoh, eel*	complaint
ricco/a	*reekoh/ah*	rich
ricetta, la	*reechetah, lah*	prescription
ricevere	*reechevehreh*	to receive
richiedere	*reekyehdehreh*	to request
riduzione, la	*reedootsyohneh, lah*	reduction
rifiutare	*reefyootahreh*	to refuse
rilassare	*reelahsahreh*	to relax
rimborso, il	*reembohrzoh, eel*	refund
rispondere	*reespondehreh*	to answer
ritardo, il	*reetahrdoh, eel*	delay
riunione, la	*reehoonyohneh, lah*	meeting
rubare	*roobahreh*	to rob
ruderi	*roodehree*	ruins (archaeological sites)

S

sala da pranzo, la	*sahlah dah prahntsoh, lah*	dining room
sapere	*sahpehreh*	to know (knowledge)
sbagliato/a	*zbahlyahtoh/ah*	wrong (mistaken)
sbrigati!	*sbreegahtee!*	hurry up!

| scale, le | *skahleh, leh* | stairs |
| scandire | *skahndeereh* | to spell |

| **lo sci** | *loh shee* | **ski** |

Italians celebrate winter with an annual **settimana bianca**, when schools close and families head to the Alps for some serious skiing.

scomodo/a	*skohmohdoh/ah*	uncomfortable
sconto, lo	*skohntoh, loh*	discount
scontrino, lo	*skontreenoh, loh*	receipt
Scozia	*skotseeyah*	Scotland
scozzese	*skotsehzeh*	Scottish
scrivere	*skreevehreh*	to write
sedia, la	*sehdeeyah, eel*	seat
sedia a rotelle, la	*sehdyah ah rohtehleh, lah*	wheelchair
segno, il	*sehnyoh, eel*	sign
sensato	*sehnsatoh*	sensible
senza	*sehntsah*	without
servire	*sehrveereh*	to serve
servizio, il	*sehrveetsyoh, eel*	service
settembre	*sehtehmbre*	September
settimana, la	*sehteemahnah, lah*	week
sgradevole	*zgrahdehvohleh*	unpleasant
sì	*see*	yes
sicuro/a	*seekooroh/ah*	safe
signora	*seenyohrah*	lady/madam
signore	*seenyohreh*	sir
silenzioso/a	*seelehntsyohzoh/ah*	quiet
sinistra	*seeneestrah*	left
sintomo, il	*seentohmoh, eel*	symptom
smettere	*smehtehreh*	to stop
soldi, i	*sohldee, ee*	money
sole, il	*sohleh, eel*	sun
sonnifero, il	*sohneefehroh, eel*	sleeping pill
sorella	*sohrehlah*	sister
sotto	*sohtoh*	below/under
spedire	*spehdeereh*	to send
spento/a	*spehntoh/ah*	off (switched)
spettacolo, lo	*spehtahkohloh, loh*	show
spiaggia, la	*spyahjah, lah*	beach

| **la spiaggia nudista** | *lah spyahjah noodeestah* | **nudist beach** |

It's common for women to go topless (or not) at all beaches, but not at swimming pools.

sporco/a	*sporkoh/ah*	dirty
sport, lo	*sport, loh*	sport
sposato/a	*spozahtoh/ah*	married
stadio, lo	*stahdeeoh, loh*	stadium

stanco/a	*stahnkoh/ah*	tired
stanza, la	*stahntsah, lah*	room
stasera	*stahsehrah*	tonight
stazione, la	*stahtsyohneh, lah*	station
stecca, la	*stehkah, lah*	carton (cigarettes)
sterlina, la	*sterleenah, lah*	sterling pound
strada, la	*strahdah, lah*	street/road
strisce (pedonali), le	*streesheh (pehdohnahlee), leh*	zebra crossing
su	*soo*	up
subito	*soobeetoh*	at once
sud	*sood*	south
suo	*soooh*	your (formal)
suonare	*swohnahreh*	to ring
svincolo, lo	*zveenkohloh, loh*	junction

T

tagliare	*tahlyahreh*	to cut
taglio, il	*tahlyoh, eel*	cut
tamponi	*tampohnee*	tampons
tardi	*tahrdee*	late (time)
tassa, la	*tahsah, lah*	tax
tassì, il	*tahsee, eel*	taxi/cab
tasso di cambio	*tahsoh dee kahmbyoh*	exchange rate
tastiera, la	*tahstyehrah, lah*	keyboard
tavola, la	*tahvohlah, lah*	table
tela, la	*tehlah, lah*	web
telefono, il	*tehlehfohnoh, eel*	telephone
telefonare	*tehlehfohnahreh*	to phone
televisione, la	*tehlehveezyohneh, lah*	television
tempo, il	*tehmpoh, eel*	time/weather
tenere	*tehnehreh*	to keep
terrazzo, il	*tehrahtsoh, eel*	terrace
tessuto, il	*tehsootoh, eel*	material (cloth)
tintoria, la	*teentohreeah, lah*	dry-cleaner's
tipico/a	*teepeekoh/ah*	typical
tipo, un	*teepoh, oon*	kind (sort)
tornare indietro	*tornareh eendyehtroh*	back (go back)
tra	*trah*	between

tradurre	***trahdooreh***	**to translate**

If you find yourself in a bind with the Italian language, most young Italians speak enough English to help you translate.

tram, il	*tram, eel*	tram
tramite	*trahmeeteh*	by (via)
treno, il	*trehnoh, eel*	train
triste	*treesteh*	sad
tu	*too*	you (informal)
tuo	*toooh*	your (informal)
tutto	*tootoh*	all

U

ufficio, il	*oofeecho, eel*	office
ufficio cambio, il	*oofeecho kahmbyoh, eel*	bureau de change
ufficio di turismo, il	*oofeecho dee tooreezmoh, eel*	tourist office
ufficio postale, il	*oofeecho pohstahleh, eel*	post office
ultimo/a, il/la	*oolteemoh/ah, eel/lah*	last
un/una	*oon/oonah*	a(n)
un altro/un'altra	*oon ahltroh/oon-ahltrah*	another
una volta	*oonah vohltah*	once
uomini	*wohmeenee*	gents
uomo, il	*wohmoh, eel*	man
urgente	*oorjehnteh*	urgent
usare	*oosahreh*	to use
uscita, la	*oosheetah, lah*	way out
uscita di sicurezza, la	*oosheetah dee seekoorehtsah, lah*	fire exit

V

va bene	*vah behneh*	ok
vacanza, la	*vahkahntsah, lah*	holiday
vaccinazione, la	*vahcheenahtsyohneh, lah*	vaccination
valido	*vahleedoh*	valid
valigia, la	*vahleejah, lah*	suitcase
valore, il	*vahlohreh, eel*	value
valuta, la	*vahlootah, lah*	currency
veicolo, il	*veheekohloh, eel*	vehicle
veloce	*vehlohche*	fast
velocemente	*vehlohchehmehnteh*	quickly
velocità	*vehlohcheetah*	speed
vendere	*vehndehreh*	to sell
venire	*vehneereh*	to come
vero/a	*vehroh/ah*	real
vero/a	*vehroh/ah*	true
vestiti, i	*vehsteetee, ee*	clothes
via	*veeah*	away
via, la	*veeyah, lah*	way (route)/road
viaggiare	*veeyahjahreh*	travel
viaggio, il	*vyahjoh, eel*	journey
vicino	*veecheenoh*	close by
vincere	*veenchereh*	to win
visita, la	*veeseetah, lah*	visit
visitare	*veeseetahreh*	to visit
visto, il	*veestoh, eel*	visa
vitamina, la	*veetahmeenah, lah*	vitamin
volere	*vohlehreh*	to want
volo, il	*vohloh, eel*	flight
vomitare	*vohmeetahreh*	to vomit

Z

zanzara, la	*tsantsahrah, lah*	mosquito

Numbers

0	**Zero**	_zehroh_
1	**Uno**	_oonoh_
2	**Due**	_dooeh_
3	**Tre**	_treh_
4	**Quattro**	_kwatroh_
5	**Cinque**	_cheenkweh_
6	**Sei**	_say_
7	**Sette**	_sehteh_
8	**Otto**	_ohtoh_
9	**Nove**	_nohveh_
10	**Dieci**	_deeyehchee_
11	**Undici**	_oondeechee_
12	**Dodici**	_dohdeechee_
13	**Tredici**	_trehdeechee_
14	**Quattordici**	_kwatordeechee_
15	**Quindici**	_kweendeechee_
16	**Sedici**	_sehdeechee_
17	**Diciasette**	_deechasehteh_
18	**Diciotto**	_deechawtoh_
19	**Diciannove**	_deechanohveh_
20	**Venti**	_vehntee_
21	**Ventuno**	_vehntoonoh_
22	**Ventidue**	_vehnteedooeh_
30	**Trenta**	_trehntah_
40	**Quaranta**	_kwahrahntah_
50	**Cinquanta**	_cheenkwantah_
60	**Sessanta**	_sessahntah_
70	**Settanta**	_sehtahntah_
80	**Ottanta**	_ohtahntah_
90	**Novanta**	_nohvahntah_
100	**Cento**	_chentoh_
1000	**Mille**	_meeleh_
1st	**Primo/a**	_preemoh/ah_
2nd	**Secondo/a**	_sehkondoh/ah_
3rd	**Terzo/a**	_tertso/a_
4th	**Quarto/a**	_kwartoh/ah_
5th	**Quinto/a**	_kweentoh/ah_

Weights & measures

gram (=0.03oz)	**grammo**	_grah_moh
100 grams	**etto**	_eh_to
kilogram (=2.2lb)	**chilo**	_kee_loh
centimetre (=0.4in)	**centimetro**	chen_tee_mehtroh
metre (=1.1yd)	**metro**	_meh_troh
kilometre (=0.6m)	**chilometro**	kee_loh_mehtroh
litre (=2.1pt)	**litro**	_lee_troh

Days & time

Monday	**Lunedì**	loone_dee_
Tuesday	**Martedì**	marteh_dee_
Wednesday	**Mercoledì**	mehrkohleh_dee_
Thursday	**Giovedì**	johveh_dee_
Friday	**Venerdì**	venehr_dee_
Saturday	**Sabato**	_sah_bahtoh
Sunday	**Domenica**	doh_mehn_eekah
What time is it?	**Che ora è?**	keh _oh_rah eh?
(Four) o'clock	**Sono (le quattro)**	sono (leh _kwah_troh)
Quarter past (six)	**(Le sei) e un quarto**	(leh say) eh oon _kwar_toh
Half past (eight)	**(Le otto) e mezzo**	(leh _oh_toh) eh _meht_sa
Quarter to (ten)	**(Le dieci) meno un quarto**	(leh _deeyeh_chee) _meh_noh oon _kwar_toh
morning	**mattina**	mah_tee_nah
afternoon	**pomeriggio**	pohmeh_ree_joh
evening	**sera**	_seh_rah
night	**notte**	_noh_teh

Clothes size conversions

Women's clothes	34	36	38	40	42	44	46	5
equiv. UK size	6	8	10	12	14	16	18	2

Men's jackets	44	46	48	50	52	54	56	5
equiv. UK size	34	36	38	40	42	44	46	4

Men's shirts	36	37	38	39	40	41	42	4
equiv. UK size	14	14.5	15	15.5	16	16.5	17	1

Shoes	36.5	37.5	39	40	41.5	42.5	44	4
equiv. UK size	4	5	6	7	8	9	10	1